BLUE
BLOOD

This book is dedicated to Manchester City Football Club – Mike Doyle
For Jaimé – David Clayton

© Mike Doyle & David Clayton 2006
This edition published 2006

The Bluecoat Press
19 Rodney Street
Liverpool L1 9EF

First Published in hardback
by The Parrs Wood Press 2004

ISBN 1 904438 38 5

BOOKS DON'T WRITE themselves and, as the writer of Mike's words, I'd like
to thank a couple of people. Firstly, to Mike Doyle – the consummate Blue and
a hero for a generation – thanks for allowing me to help write your story.
Thanks to Andy Searle at The Parrs Wood Press for publishing the hardback
edition, which was so successful, and to Colin Wilkinson of The Bluecoat
Press for publishing this paperback edition. Thanks to Cheryl and Scott Doyle
for their help and insights along the way, and in particular to Grant Doyle,
whose love for his dad is all too clear and without whom this book may never
have been possible. At my end, I'd like to thank Simon Thorley for designing
the cover and to Johnny Hart for writing the foreword. To James H Reeve for
a priceless quote (does he do any other kind?) and for anyone else who has
recounted tales about Mike's time at Maine Road, particularly Peter Gardener,
the former Evening News sports writer, for championing the young Doyle
when he was an unknown youngster. Finally, to my mum, for taking me to
watch City in the first place and my dad for being the first in a long line of
Blues. Thanks to all my family, but especially my wife Sarah, who has put up
with me disappearing to Ashton for hours on end each week and supported
me throughout. Finally, thanks and all the love I have to my little boy Harry
and his baby sisters Jaimé and Chrissie. I'll make up those lost play hours over
the next few months. That's a promise.

BLUE
BLOOD
The Mike Doyle Story

Mike Doyle
David Clayton

The Bluecoat Press

CONTENTS

FOREWORD

BY JOHNNY HART

FROM DAY ONE, Michael was what I called a 'City punter'. He was single-minded and knew where he wanted to go and gave the club the utmost from the start of his career to the finish. He was a City stalwart through and through and, if any player's blood did run Blue, it was Mike Doyle's.

He wouldn't have a bad word said about the club back in his playing days and I doubt he's any different today. In fact, I know he's not!

He made more than 500 appearances for the Blues and he pulled his guts out every time he played and was a good, honest player. You don't win international caps if you aren't a good player and you can add to that a clutch of winner's medals, too. He had City at heart and I was proud to watch him develop from a skinny kid into an England player.

My memory has robbed me of the time when he first arrived on the ground staff but I do recall him making his debut against Cardiff City back in 1965. He was only a young lad but he handled the situation well and showed he had a good head on his shoulders. He played a few more games that season and it wasn't long before he was a first team regular.

He looked at me as a sort of father figure, I suppose, and even until just recently, he still talked to me the same way as he did when he was a youngster. I was on the coaching staff when he broke through and I looked out for him, as I did all the lads, and I prided myself in being there for them when they needed me.

There were times when I backed him up when he was in trouble and there were times when I helped cool him down, too, when the occasion demanded. I remember being sat on the bench with our sub Derek Jeffries when Colin Bell picked up an injury with around 20 minutes to go in one particular match. We were attacking the Platt Lane and Colin had to come off so I told Jeffries he was going on.

"There you go," I said to him. "This is your chance."

"Where do you want me to play?" he asked.

"In front of Doyley and just behind Neil Young on the left," I replied.

"Right-oh, I'll do that," he said and ran over to the far side of the pitch. Within a few seconds Doyley grabbed him by the scruff of the neck and looked like he was going to whack him one. After the match I asked Mike what it was all about.

"The little git," growled Mike. "I asked him where he was going to play and he said 'Well, Harty says I'm a better player than you and told me to take your place and push you up front'. So I told him I was going to kill him."

You didn't mess around with Mike, especially when he was going about his business on the pitch. In my opinion, if you were good and honest on the field you attracted people around you and that's how Mike was.

There was another time that typified his character and how he lived his life. It happened in Australia when we were touring and we were being covered by an obnoxious local journalist who, in most people's opinion was pushing his luck with the way he acted and the things he wrote.

At a presentation dinner, he openly claimed that City were "not fit to burn," and was constantly ragging us, saying we weren't a good side and had only won the league through luck.

This one particular evening, there was a toast to the Queen and the Duke of Lancaster. We all stood up and toasted Her Majesty – all except this journalist who muttered "Stuff the Queen." I'd had enough of him and his arrogance and was unfortunate enough to be sat next to him. "Pass the sugar," he blurted shortly after. No please or thank you, so I told him to get stuffed, too.

7

Word got around as to what he'd said during the toast and I noticed one or two players talking about him. If a kangaroo court was in session, this was the right country to hold it in!

This bloke eventually went to the toilet and him going made me want to go, too. As I approached the toilet, the journalist flew out of the door in front of me – his nose busted and covered in blood. Stood over him was Doyley.

"Don't you call my Queen," he snarled. I stopped him administrating any more 'justice' and told him to get on the coach immediately whilst I saw to the injured party. I took the bloke back into the toilets and swabbed him down. I told him he'd had it coming and not to speak about the Queen like he had done in front of our lads – least of all Mike Doyle!

Mike got away with it, though.

Doyley was a hard man on and off the pitch but he was a bloody good player, too. He was intelligent and honest and you couldn't ask for more from him because he always gave 150 per cent once he pulled on the sky blue jersey. He captained the team and represented his country, too, and though he should have perhaps earned more caps than he did, I doubt there were many prouder of wearing the three lions on his chest than Michael Doyle.

He lived and breathed Manchester City during his playing career. What more could you ask for from a player?

With Mike, what you saw is what you got.

INTRODUCTION

THIS BOOK IS all about my life and times as a footballer, from my days with Reddish Vale, to the incredible highs of life with my boyhood idols Manchester City, and subsequently my stays with Stoke City, Bolton and Rochdale. It is an insight into what made me tick and I've tried to be as candid as possible. Some of you won't agree with certain things I have to say along the way, but that's life. I've always spoken my mind and I'm not going to change now. My first book, My Team was released in 1977, but there were a lot of things I couldn't say at the time and many stories I was unable to recount. Time has moved on and everything I had to leave out from that book has been included in *Blue Blood* plus all that's happened since. I hope it brings back a few happy memories. This is a fully revised and updated paperback edition with more added plus a new chapter. I hope you enjoy reading it.

Mike Doyle
October 2005

I FIRST READ *Manchester City: My Team* by Mike Doyle back in 1994 when a work colleague passed it on to me to read. I was a Blue and here was a book on a Blue legend – it all made sense. It took me about a week to finish and though I knew a few others wanted to read it, I decided to keep it for myself. I just had a feeling it would come in useful again someday. About eight years later, I dug it out and read it again. I thought that for someone with Mike Doyle's reputation for speaking his mind, it was a little timid in parts.

And that got me thinking. What had happened to Mike Doyle since he hung his boots up? Had he said all that he'd wanted to when the first book came out in 1977? Probably not, seeing he was still a City player and therefore restricted in what he could say. I did a bit of digging around but hardly anyone had seen him in years. He never attended supporters meetings, never took part in the match-day hospitality like many other former players did but nobody knew why. I wanted to find out more.

After a few weeks trying to get a telephone number, I decided to put the idea of tracking Mike Doyle down on the backburner. I had enough to be getting on with editing the *City Magazine*. Then, I was at Maine Road waiting to chat to Kevin Cummins about his photographic project entitled *We're Not Really Here*. He was a few minutes late because he was with a group of former players who were signing autograph sheets for a special collector's edition of the book.

You can probably see where this is leading … one of those players was Mike Doyle. As he passed me on the stairs I asked him if he would like to chat about possibly updating his original autobiography. He said he would think about it and passed me his number.

Two months later, we finally met up and talked. He admitted there was a lot of stuff he couldn't say back then and I could tell that it had also been written not quite as candidly as Mike expressed himself in reality. I met with publisher Andy Searle at Parrs Wood Press and he was very interested in revising and updating *My Team* and soon after, the contracts were drawn up and duly signed by all parties.

Titles were suggested such as *Local Hero* and suchlike but I felt *Blue Blood* said everything about Mike Doyle that needed to be said. Here was a player who gave his all for City and was fiercely proud to pull on the sky blue shirt throughout his 15-year stay. They were his boyhood heroes and he was living the dream every single day he was at Maine Road. He never shirked responsibility and regularly spilled blood for the cause.

He was forthright in his opinions and he wound the Manchester United fans up as often and as easily as he pleased and then backed up his words on the pitch as City pummelled their old rivals season after season. He received death threats, had his windows put in and tyres slashed – all because he loved the Blues and hated the Reds.

I pored over the original book and decided there was still plenty in there that would be interesting to include, so long as it was revised and where possible, added to. There are many stories and incidents that couldn't be printed first time around and I've added the colourful language Mike uses on occasion! Let's face it, he's not one to say 'flipping hell' when he could use a more, shall we say, colourful expression. If you plan to let your kids read this, make sure you're okay with the expletives, first.

I've put in quotes before each chapter that give you a feel of how Mike was at the time and how others saw him. This is a snapshot of a player's life and in this case, he just happens to be one of the greatest players Manchester City have ever employed and, he is still the last captain to lift a knockout trophy, some 30 years on, though that's one record he'll be happy to pass on.

There are fantastic highs and incredible lows along the way. Now fasten your seatbelt, sit back and relax as best you can. You're in for a bumpy ride.

David Clayton
October 2005

SELECTED MIKE DOYLE QUOTES

If I had to pack the game in tomorrow I would go straight out and buy a season ticket for Maine Road. And I would be there at the reserve, youth team and bounce games. I grew up in a town that only wanted to know Manchester United and I've been lucky enough to help change that.

Let's face it, I'm a City fanatic. I'm the guy on the terraces who has been given the chance to put down his rattle and step out for the team he loves.

I know my strengths and my limitations. I never hide. I never shirk responsibility. People have said to me that I should play for England. I never lose sleep about that. I'm just happy to play for Manchester City.

MARCH 1974

I still feel the same way about Manchester United as I did when my school-mates used to ram it down my throat that City were second best. I want to play in this game against them and then the two League Cup semi-final legs against them … even if it kills me.

NOVEMBER 1969

Mike Doyle? I was standing next to him outside Maine Road after the Marsh/captaincy row and saw a little bloke with a terrible wig take a swing at him. Doyley blocked the punch and offered to take the bloke into the gym if he wanted a scrap. Imagine my surprise at reading in the Mirror on the Monday "Doyle threatens fan"! The bloke naturally declined, but Doyley took a woman on one side in the old car park and obviously told her the story about what had gone on. Gospel truth, that.

JAMES H REEVE, NOVEMBER 2003

1

Raw

Boys Find New Marksman
(Manchester Evening News, 1961)
Mr Leslie McDowall and Mr George Poyser, the Manchester City manager and his assistant, watched Stockport Boys beat Clwyd and Conway Boys 7-0 at Edgeley Park on Monday evening. Possibly they were there to confirm the report of one of their scouts, an ex-Stockport County player, on Mike Doyle, the Stockport left half.

IT'S FAIR TO SAY that when I took out my notepad to write a letter to my local paper, I had no idea of the impact the results of it being published would have in my life. Kids often have grand ideas for the future and what they would like to be when they grow up and I was no different. So, at the tender age of ten, I posted my dreams in an envelope and pretty much forgot about it.

I wasn't a bookworm or a serial letter writer. The reasons for my scribe were purely financial – the *Manchester Evening News* had invited youngsters to write in and say what career they hoped to follow when they left school. I think there was a £1 prize for every letter published and that was certainly an incentive so far as I was concerned.

I wrote and told the editor – and anyone else who cared to read my letter – that I had every intention of becoming a professional footballer or, at worst a physical education instructor. Sport would feature highly, of that I was absolutely definite.

But that letter was read by someone who would play a large role in helping me achieve those dreams and for that, I will be forever in his debt. Harry Godwin, the man who was

Manchester City's chief scout for many years, signed dozens of youngsters who made their mark in top-class football. Harry died several years ago but he remains one of City's genuine unsung heroes. It transpired that I was one of his 'finds' and one of Harry's favourite stories concerned the 'detective' work he did on me. It began after he cut out my letter from the paper and put it with a few other clippings he had taken from various papers for one reason or another.

As Harry was fond of relating, my letter was fairly brief, but very much to the point: 'I'm not much interested in mathematics or English, or school work in general but I AM determined to become a professional footballer or a PE instructor.' Harry read the letter, smiled to himself, then clipped it from the paper and put it away in an old green diary. The cutting gave my address and after that I pretty much forgot about it.

Nothing dramatic happened after my letter was printed. There was no queue of scouts watching me play or offering lucrative deals for this hoped star of the future although, as a kid, a part of you really believes that might happen and why not? We all have our dreams and I just happened to share mine with around one million readers of the local paper. The lucrative deals could wait, though in truth, some 25 years after retirement from the game, I'm still waiting.

Time passed; in fact, something like four years went by. Then, one day, Harry Godwin went along to watch Stockport Boys playing Stretford Boys at the Ship Canal Ground at Stretford. The Stockport Boys left back took his eye and when he enquired about the lad's name he was told his name was Mike Doyle. There was something familiar to Harry about that name but it still took him a weekend of puzzling over things before it clicked and he found the diary. Charlie Gee, the chief scout at Maine Road before Harry took over, had been watching my career develop and was a good friend of my dad and he had

14

told Harry to pay me a visit. He told Harry that Michael Doyle would be signing for City because he'd already agreed as much with my dad! It was all signed and sealed and I hadn't a clue about anything.

In the meantime, quite a few other people had noted my name as well and a scout from Manchester United was trailing me – what a waste of time that was, for that is one club I would have never joined given my family's loyalties. My dad Tommy would have disowned me as a son if I had talked with the Reds. In fact, I was virtually brought up behind the Kippax at my grandparents' home on Deramore Street.

Burnley, Stoke City, Everton, Tottenham, Arsenal, Liverpool, Newcastle United and Wolves watched my progress closely, too. Yet, when I left school it was Wolves who invited me down to have a look at their ground and have a chat about a possible deal. They were a fair side back then so I went to the Black Country with my parents and another lad from Stockport Boys, Tony Dove. I was a bit starry-eyed when Wolves sought me out and it wouldn't have taken much for Tony and me to sign on the dotted line straight away had we been alone.

Wolves were very good and they showed us around the ground and treated us to a meal. I'd been impressed by the training facilities and with the sun shining on my back I got taken in by it all, but my dad Tommy hadn't. No wonder, either, with the crafty sod arranging my future for me! He didn't give much away to our hosts because he knew something few others did. So I still hadn't signed for anyone when I left Molineux later that day. Wolves were ready to take the gamble, but it was actually my mum who used delaying tactics – she advised me to think things over for a couple of days, before committing myself. Stoke City then made their move for me (the first of several during my career as it happened) and even offered my mum a washing machine! Her face lit up and I think if she could have signed my name for me she would have done there and then, but dad again remained pokerfaced and unimpressed about it all. Forty-eight hours later, Harry Godwin entered my life.

He called round at my home and as he was passing the window he could see that lying on the table was a policeman's helmet – my dad's – and a Manchester City programme. He felt reassured about the City interest and happier still when my mum invited him in. In those days there was a great deal of talk about youngsters – or, rather, their parents – being offered all sorts of incentives to get their kids to sign for clubs. There was talk of cars, washing machines and the like.

Harry Godwin offered me nothing more than honesty and a dream of playing for my boyhood heroes. He was utterly down-to-earth in his approach and informed me that washing machines, television sets and so on do not make a professional footballer – the only thing that can make a footballer is the lad himself. It was the first time anybody had spoken to me honestly and what he said made perfect sense and I knew then that I was going to learn my trade at Maine Road.

I was disciplined as a young lad with a copper for a dad, which was fine by me, but not so popular with some of the pond life I came into contact with in my neighbourhood. We lived on a council estate and I used to get terrible stick about dad's profession and was beaten up on several occasions because of it by local bullies. My dad took me to a police training academy to learn unarmed combat when I was about 14 but I was still going when I was 20, though I never told anyone at City. I learned to try and pacify rather than dive in and I think had a definite effect on the type of player I became – I was never afraid of pain, but I suppose there were a few occasions in my career when the pacifying skills went out of the window.

It was 1962 when I realised my boyhood dream and signed for City. I became a ground-staff assistant, along with a couple of other lads from Stockport Boys. My allegiance to the club was total. The only twinge of doubt I had about the wisdom of my decision came on the Saturday before I reported for my first day with the Blues. I had been with some pals to a holiday camp in North Wales and when we were returning home on the Saturday we tuned in for the football results. Ironically for me, City had been playing at Molineux – and Wolves had given us an 8-1 hammering. There was a lad with us, Harry Jones, and bloody hell was he giving it out. I wondered for a moment if I'd made the right decision but then decided my employers would be keen for new defensive talent to come through the ranks sooner rather than later. Take positives out of a negative – that was my maxim back then and still is today.

The following Monday, I reported to Maine Road where Johnny Hart and Fred Tilson gave me the job of cleaning boots with Bobby Cunliffe. While I was brushing away, Bert Trautmann, City's legendary goalkeeper walked in. He said: "Have you cleaned my boots?" I said I had and passed them to him. "Very nice job," he said examining them." He had this wonderful German accent and seemed a lovely bloke but, legend or not I was a cocky bugger and I couldn't help myself. I asked him, 'How's your back, by the way?', in reference to his having had to pick the ball out of the net eight times the previous Saturday. He didn't say anything and left the room. I continued cleaning other boots and it wasn't until about 20 minutes later that he came back into the boot room, washed and dressed. He got me by the collar and picked me up and said: "You show fucking respect! You don't speak to me ever again like that." I apologised and, if truth be told, was close to tears at the time – I was being scalded, deservedly so, by one of the game's most respected professionals and I was no more than a scrawny kid who had achieved exactly nothing

The Volkswagen Beetle had just come out and Bert had a bright yellow one and I got to know that car very well because

I ended up washing it every day throughout the season – I had no choice. A lesson learned but it only made me respect Bert even more. He was one of the best looking blokes I've ever seen and always reminded me of Kurt Jurgen, the German film star. Not long after that incident in the boot room, I got into the reserves and Bert was in goal. He came over to me and held out his hand, which I shook. "Everything is forgotten, now," he said. "What?" I replied incredulously. "You know what I'm talking about," he replied. I nodded and smiled. "If you keep the attitude that you've got now," he said, "you will become a good footballer." That was my debut and we played Bolton Wanderers who beat us 5-1 and if it hadn't been for Bert we'd have lost about 20-1 – no exaggeration.

At that time the City team had some of the game's biggest names despite the club being in the Second Division. Apart from Bert Trautmann, there were two Scots, Alex Harley and Matt Gray, who had both played for Third Lanark north of the Border and made their name as forwards there. Another was Peter Dobing, who later captained Stoke to victory in a League Cup final and there were Joe Hayes, George Hannah, Cliff Sear, Colin Barlow, Bill Leivers, Bobby Kennedy, David Wagstaffe and young hopefuls such as Alan Oakes, Paul Aimson and Vic Gomersall.

For ground-staff lads like me, the routine was straightforward enough – and not really what I had expected. Come to that, team manager Les McDowall, a dour Scot, wasn't what I had expected, either. Not that I ever saw much of him, but when I did he was always immaculately dressed in a smart suit and not the tracksuit I had first envisaged. As for the routine, soccer seemed to come a good second, for I would arrive at the ground around 9am, put the playing kit out, clean the boots, sweep the dressing-rooms and clean the toilets and help out on the ground as well, mostly sweeping the terraces. I also became an expert snooker player during my ample spare time.

The first team squad didn't report for training until about 11am and once we youngsters had got the kit out and done our chores, we would nip into the recreation room and get involved in a game of snooker. It would be a quick game early on, another session between 12.30pm and 2.30pm, after the morning training, then an afternoon game of skittle ball in the gym and back to the snooker table until around 5 o'clock, when it was time to catch the bus home. This was the daily routine during my first 12 months as a Manchester City youth player and I sometimes used to reflect that if I didn't make the grade in professional football, there would probably be a career for me as the Jimmy White of my day.

The youngsters rarely outwitted the older players and a perfect example of this was during one of the numerous training sessions we had in Wythenshawe Park. We jogged from Platt Lane to the park and when we got there, we legged it around the perimeter before heading back up Princess Parkway along the grass verge. There were a few of the younger lads out at the front and there were still a lot of the older players at the club at the time such as Gray and Harley, but they were nowhere to be seen. It was this way on a few occasions and then one day we saw them pass us – on the top deck of a passing No.42 bus! They obviously beat us back and then we got a bollocking for not being as fit as the older lads.

One of the men with whom I came into closest contact at that time was Johnny Hart, a former player who was on the backroom staff who took me under his wing. Later he became manager of City for a short time before ill health forced him out of the game. I used to feel that Johnny was one of the few people who would take the time and trouble to talk to you at length about the game in general, and about your own game in particular. He hadn't been a wing-half himself – he played up front – but many a time he would take me on one side and give me the benefit of his advice. It was something I valued then and still do – for me, Johnny Hart was the epitome of loyalty and I say that believing with all my heart that loyalty to your club is of the greatest importance. I never wanted to leave Manchester City, in spite of some traumatic moments in the club's life and my own … and I always hoped I would be a one-club player and that should have been the case. But things don't always turn out the way you want them to, do they?

As a kid, I found Johnny a real father figure, but he could make you jump when he felt it necessary. He didn't like to see the young players smoking in the dressing room and we all knew it – though once or twice some of the lads tried to pull a fast one. I remember one day Neil Young and David Wagstaffe were having a crafty fag and Johnny crept up behind the door. He could obviously smell the smoke inside the dressing room and the next thing that happened, Johnny appeared. Both players immediately jumped to their feet and slipped their hands into their trousers pockets. Johnny knew what was going on – so he simply kept them standing there talking for several minutes, while all the time those cigarettes were almost burning a hole in the lads' trousers. Eventually, smoke started to spiral from Youngy's pocket, a small brown hole appeared where the cigarette had burned and suddenly Waggy let out a scream – his cigarette had burned his fingers. Johnny then walked out, chuckling to himself.

Before match days, we had to have the dressing-rooms looking spick and span. In fact, it was not uncommon to see Johnny or Jimmy Meadows walk in and rub a finger across the mirror, or over a bench or a table, to see if there was a speck of dust in true sergeant major style. If there was any dust, you might find yourself ordered back to the ground on a Tuesday or a Thursday night for an extra training stint. I got a day off every week to attend school, where I was enrolled to take a course in mechanical engineering. I soon decided I couldn't stick it, so I told my mum I'd go to night school two nights a week instead. I went three times to Stockport Technical College – then I played hooky and went instead to a local gym where I took part in five-a-side football matches. I carried my notebook and textbooks around with me and while I was playing five-a-side I had a mate copying notes from the textbook into my exercise book, so that my mum would think I'd really been studying at night school. That used to cost me a bob or two, because my pal wasn't going to be the mug for nothing, but it was money well spent.

As a schoolboy footballer, I used to get into trouble quite a lot with referees – a habit I've never quite managed to break. After I had joined City, Johnny Hart would talk to me about my game and tell me: 'All right, you've got to learn to play it by the book … but never let this curb your enthusiasm for the game, or your aggression. If you retain those qualities, you have a good chance of making the grade.' Harry Godwin, too, on the day he talked me into signing for City, made one simple point: 'The only thing I'll promise you is that if you work hard at it, you'll get your chance.' And I did. I also learned that if I thought I could be enthusiastic and aggressive, there were other characters around who could be just as uncompromising. In the gym one day, four of the youngsters, me included, were up against Jimmy Meadows, Johnny Hart and Bobby Cunliffe in a game of skittle ball. I stood around five feet six inches tall and weighed maybe seven and a half stone at that time and on the wall of the gym there was a hook, planted about six feet above ground level. Jimmy Meadows was a built like a brick shit house and he really whacked me during that game. I shot off the floor as if I'd been rocket-propelled and finished up hanging by my tracksuit top from that hook on the wall, with my feet six inches from the ground. Glyn Pardoe had to lift me down.

The next day, we were having another session and Jimmy Meadows whacked me again – only this time, I didn't shoot up in the air; I went down on the ground, laid out cold. They carried me to the treatment room and I was just coming round when Johnny Hart appeared. He saw that I wasn't going to die and said to me: 'You'll not find it quite as hard, once you've put a bit of weight on.'

One of my closest pals then was Glyn Pardoe, whom we called 'Solly'. We'd seen a film in which one of the characters was an Arab, complete with fez and he was the spitting image of Glyn, dark and swarthy, so Glyn became 'Solly' after that. One player who wasn't quite such a close buddy, but I'll not name him because there are certain players supporters want to believe was an icon and I'm not going to be the one to ruin a player's reputation just because we didn't get on. Anyway, this guy was put in his place by a man who later became the manager of City – Ron Saunders. At that time, Saunders was playing for Portsmouth and our young hopeful was in direct opposition to him that day. Johnny Hart gave our lad some good advice: 'Ron Saunders may be knocking on a bit as a player, but he's been around and he can still do his stuff. So watch out for him – don't think he's a soft touch.' The young player sniffed scornfully and said he'd put this Saunders 'in his pocket'. Pompey won 2-0 that day and Saunders scored a good goal. He didn't mouth off quite so much after that.

I got my first taste of football playing for the 'B' team on a Saturday and for a short spell was in at right back. Then I made the switch to right half and I wore the No. 4 jersey from then on. I still played at fullback for the youth side, though – simply because City hadn't got anyone else to do the job. There were many times during my City career that I filled in when there were no other volunteers – once against Arsenal we won a penalty. Franny was out so Rodney Marsh was supposed to take it, but he didn't fancy it. Colin Bell was next in line but he didn't feel confident. It was getting ridiculous so I picked the ball up, placed on the spot and blazed it over! A couple of times I even ended up in nets when our goalkeeper was injured, again because nobody else would do it. That was all to come, though, and I was still a wet-nosed kid who was full of hope and enthusiasm. It wasn't long before I moved up to the 'A' team and, after nine matches in that grade, I made my debut in the reserves, at Bolton. I was 15 years old and playing in the same side as Trautmann and Wagstaffe – not bad company for a scrawny kid from a rough estate.

Apart from that promotion, the pattern was the same as before. As for the training in those days, it was far removed from the sort of stuff we do now. There was absolutely no sophistication about it – we would go out and get under starter's orders which meant 15 or 20 laps around the pitch as a warm-up. There were no sprints; you simply ran and lapped and that was it. Once a week, the reserves (or 'stiffs', as they were better known amongst the lads) played a game against the first team – and there was no way that game would end until the seniors had won. Sometimes a game would go on for two and a half hours and I remember one occasion when our goalkeeper, Steve Fleet, called to trainer Jimmy Meadows: 'You'll have to get a clocking-in card … because we're not going to be beaten today. This is going to be a nine till five job.'

As my career with City flourished in later years, I always felt sorry for Steve Fleet – he was a nice lad and unlucky to have had Bert Trautmann in front of him and then Joe Corrigan, who went from being the worst goalkeeper I had ever played with to the best. When Joe was bad, he was awful but when he was good, he was amongst the best in the world.

In one match, we were murdering Burnley at Turf Moor but we hadn't scored. Then one of Colin Bell's mates, Colin Waldron, of all people, hit a 40-yard ball that I was about to head clear but Joe shouted for me to leave it. I moved out of the way and glanced around in time to see it go through his legs and into the net. Later in the game, Joe shouted at his sparring partner Tommy Booth to pass the ball back which he did. The ball somehow again went through his legs but he tried to reach through instead of turning around and a Burnley player slid in to just send the ball over the line. Joe had scrambled back, slid into the net and got his feet entangled in the netting and lay there, stranded on his back. Tommy turned to me and said, "Look at him. He looks like a fucking beached whale." To be fair to Joe, that was without doubt his lowest ebb. Call it fate in Joe's case but his career path was about to change. Big Joe was a drinker and an eater and was well overweight, probably as much as three stone, when he broke his jaw and had it wired up. He didn't tell us how he'd done it be we all reckoned he'd been in a punch-up but him being the bully on the pitch and such a big lad, he wouldn't actually admit to that. He was training on his own for a while and when he returned to the squad a few months later he looked like a real athlete – it was an incredible transformation.

2

MIXING IT WITH THE BEST OF THEM

DOYLE'S DAZZLING DEBUT
(DAILY EXPRESS, 12TH MARCH 1965)

It was a night to remember for 18-year old Mike Doyle who made his League debut at wing half for Manchester City because of an eye injury to Alan Oakes. Doyle was given plenty to think about by the Cardiff attack but he turned in a competent display and helped an enterprising Manchester City win a point.

AT LEAST PLAYING for the reserves was more my idea of what I should be doing as a professional footballer. But after just two years' cutting my teeth with the stiffs I was staggered to find myself in the first team, for a game at Cardiff. What should have been my most exciting day almost became a complete disaster when I came close to missing my debut thanks to a few crossed wires. Alan Oakes, who had already got into the side, had to cry off at the last moment because he had a boil over his eye. It was a midweek match and the rest of first team had already left for the airport, when Jimmy Meadows pulled me out of training with the reserves to say: 'You're playing tonight.' I thought he was joking – after all, the first team squad had got bathed, changed and left to catch the plane to Cardiff. He had to be kidding, didn't he? 'Be at the airport at 2pm,' were his final instructions and it was 11.45am by the time I had got changed, bathed and dressed. There was no chauffeur waiting to speed to me the airport as would happen to the players of today – it was make your own way if you want to play – what the present day youngsters would call a case of 'keeping it real'! But I definitely did want to play.

This was my chance to show the boss that I could hack it at the top and I wasn't going to let it pass me by.

There was much to do because I had to go home, which meant four busses from Maine Road. I caught a bus along Lloyd Street to Great Western Street, then got the No.53 from Great Western Street to Belle Vue, then the 77 to the Bull's Head pub at Reddish. Then it was a No.17 to the top of the road where I lived and I still had to run a mile and a half to reach my front door. If anyone ever wondered how I managed to maintain a high level of fitness during my playing career perhaps my journey to and from the club each day helps explain a lot!

By the time I got home, it was almost one o'clock. When I told my mum I was playing at Cardiff that night, she didn't believe me. Finally I convinced her and she decided that I needed some sustenance, so she parcelled up a pile of sandwiches and some cake and told me to make sure I ate the lot, bless her. I was running up Longford Road, hoping I could get a bus, which would take me close enough to the airport. Along the way, I saw an old mongrel dog that looked as if it could do with a few crumbs in his belly, so I unwrapped the sandwiches and cake and gave the lot to him. He seemed happy enough with his part of the deal.

I reached the bus stop, but no there was no sign of the bus, so I waited … and waited. I began to panic and then a passing woman informed the buses were on strike from one o'clock. I thought 'For fuck's sake! Just my bloody luck.' I had a pile of change in my pocket and went in search of a phone box. There was no directory in the box I found and I didn't even know the number of the club. Fate was seemingly conspiring against me and when Joey Barton had his shirt stolen moments before he was about to make his City debut at Middlesbrough a few years back, it brought memories of my first game flooding back. Just then I heard a car slowing down and as I looked out

I saw my old mate Vic Gomersall. 'What's happening?' he asked. I told him I was down to make my debut at Cardiff that night, but that it looked as if I was going to miss the plane. Vic said: 'Are you fucking serious?' Then he said 'Hop in – I'll run you there.' We got to Ringway with about five minutes to spare. I was going to the ball after all.

The lads were great and many of them has a quiet word with me, offering advice and what to expect but it wasn't until I was in the tunnel at Ninian Park and I saw John Charles waiting slightly ahead of me that the occasion began to sink in. Charles was a man mountain with thighs the size of tree trunks and I couldn't help thinking that if he smashed into me he'd snap me in half. I learned a lot in that match and some of the things I witnessed on my debut helped me prepare for the many tough encounters that lay before me. I found out for the first time what people meant when they talked about players going 'over the top'. Cardiff had John Charles and Ivor Allchurch playing for them and I was a bit dazzled to think I was on the same field as these two international stars. But 'King John', who was playing on the right-hand side in the middle of the park, was still a real professional, even if he had had his best years in the game and when he and I tangled, I came off worst.

At 17, I was still rather skinny and I wasn't tall. John Charles seemed like a bulldozer to me as he came in for the ball. Twice he hit me and I felt as if I'd been knocked down by a car, no doubt keen to scare me out of the match. Each time I went into the tackle with him he trampled all over me. After the second tackle, as I lay on the floor, our Irish international inside-forward Johnny Crossan, who was vastly more experienced than I was and half the size of Charles said: 'Don't worry, I'll take care of him.' I gaped a bit, because Johnny wasn't even as big as me ... but I was in complete awe when I saw him take on John Charles. He took the ball almost up to the big fellow, kicked it forward a yard or two, so that Charles committed himself – then he seemed to run right up Charles's leg, not stopping until he'd reached the thigh. As Charles lay writhing on the ground, my team-mate looked down at him and said: 'Come on, get up, you big Welsh tosser!' It wasn't as bad as it looked because big John was soon back in the action again, but to my innocent eyes it seemed as if Crossan had almost got away with murder – for an impressionable kid he'd also gone to hero status in about 5 seconds flat.

We drew 2-2 that night in front of around 30,000 people and I cleared the ball off the line in injury time but instead of hoofing it away, I chested it down and laid it to the 'keeper. After the game Johnny Hart asked why I hadn't got rid of the ball and I told him because there was no need. He couldn't believe I'd been so calm, especially seeing as it was on my debut. I felt I had turned in a fair performance, although I knew that for me this was only the start. I had to show I could stay the pace. That game at Cardiff was shortly before Easter and, by the time the end of the season was approaching, we were without a manager, for George Poyser, former boss Les McDowall's successor, had left the club.

On the Easter Monday, we were due to play Coventry City at Maine Road and the entire City team was in the melting pot. In fact, you could expect to go into the dressing room and see 18 to 20 names on the sheet that was pinned up telling who should report for duty on match days. The club, at that stage, was going through one of its worst spells since I had joined and, at times, I had the feeling that the we were like a ship without a rudder.

Poyser had been the chief scout before stepping up to the managerial chair. He was well enough like but, despite all his efforts to get the team playing football, it had become clear that time was running out. There was one incident, shortly before the end of his time at Maine Road, which summed it all up for me and made me pissed off not only with some of my team-mates, but with the club for allowing things to reach the stage where such a situation could happen. George presented the image of a middle-aged, pipe-smoking character who said very little, although he often looked pensive. We'd never seen him in a tracksuit and we didn't expect to do so, either.

One day, however, he turned up during a training session clad in a tracksuit that didn't fit him and wearing a pair of brown brogues! He may well have had a suit on underneath, too and with the greatest respect in the world, he looked a complete berk. His appearance was the signal for a chorus of laughter and some none-too-flattering remarks from Waggy and Youngy. "Fuckin' hell!" said one of them, "Nothing fucking fits him!" Amusing though it was, it was a sad fact that if players could show such disrespect to the man they were meant to be sweating blood for out on the pitch, there was something badly wrong with things at the club.

After George had gone, City were in a state of limbo for a while and it was on that Easter Monday that I experienced a sample of the lack of cohesion and liaison within the club between the various departments. I was standing on the steps at Maine Road, about an hour before kick-off eating fish and chips – not the sort of thing you would expect to see David James or Nedum Onuoha doing these days – and minding my own business. Suddenly, I felt a tap on my shoulder from behind and when I turned round there was a dapper little white-haired fellow.

"Go in and get changed – you're playing today." He then made his way up the steps and disappeared through the doorway.

I was staggered and turned to one of my mates. 'Did you hear what he said?' I asked. He looked as surprised as I was because, although I'd never talked to the little man before and had seldom seen him around, I still recognised him. He was the chairman, Albert Alexander. Even at that, I didn't feel I could take his word for it that I was playing, so I went inside and met Johnny Hart in the dressing room. 'I've just seen the chairman and he's told me I'm playing against Coventry. Is it true?' I asked. And Johnny looked at me and said: 'Didn't you know you were playing?' I took that to be a 'yes' and got stripped and changed. I was hoping the half-eaten chips wouldn't lie too heavily in my stomach, as it wasn't exactly the greatest pre-match meal I could have had.

But that was the sort of thing that could and did happen at City in those days. Everything seemed to be done in a slapdash fashion and there appeared to be little rhyme or reason about decisions that were taken. I must stress here that Albert Alexander did as much for the club as any man and Manchester City was his life. At that time I didn't know – and wouldn't have bothered my head if I had known – about differences of opinion in the boardroom and the chairman, a gentleman in every respect, certainly did his utmost to keep things on an even keel. Before he had finished, he had achieved something, too, because he recognised that the time had come for action.

It wasn't merely that the club were in the Second Division and trying to climb back into the First; they had to compete with the glamour of Manchester United and, at that point in time, City were running a very poor second, both in terms of results and of pulling power at the turnstiles. Albert Alexander was nobody's fool, even if he was quiet in his ways, and he had his own ideas about putting matters to rights. He was instrumental, I have always believed, in initiating the moves that led to Joe Mercer and Malcolm Allison teaming up together at Maine Road and if that's the case, he left quite a legacy.

That day against Coventry, City pitched the youngsters in and besides myself, there were Glyn Pardoe, Dave Connor and Alf Wood and we acquitted ourselves pretty well, drawing 2-2

– the same score as my debut match at Cardiff. The next day we played away against Crystal Palace and we were winning up until virtually the last kick of the game when the Eagles finally stuck the ball in our net. That also meant my record now read three games played, three games drawn – at least we'd remained unbeaten but, by the same token, I was still awaiting my first victory in a sky blue jersey.

City had been relegated the previous season but had failed to bounce back at the first attempt by the end of the campaign, so I decided to take a break away from Manchester and headed for Torquay with a few of my City team-mates, taking on a job for the summer at the popular holiday resort. Harry Dowd used to go there in the pre-season but I can honestly say that driving 300 miles on A-roads to Devon in a mini packed with four big sweaty blokes and a load of luggage was not much fun, but we made it eventually. We had jobs pushing pedaloes and motor boats into the sea for the holidaymakers and the good thing about it was that the chap who was in charge of the beaches was a former chief constable from Manchester who knew my dad, so he sort of looked out for me. In the evenings, it was our job to tie all the boats up ready for the next day and, one particular night, we were out in the water gathering the boats together when we were surrounded by what we thought were sharks – we almost crapped ourselves! They turned out to be dolphins but believe me, in the failing light, they looked anything but friendly. I suppose you had to be there, really.

It was a great time for me. I was 16-years-old and had my whole life ahead of me. I was playing for the club I loved and being paid for it, though I was never going to be rich on the basic wage I was on. I also met Mike Summerbee whilst I was down there and it was the start of a great friendship that would see him living at my parents' house when he first signed for City and continuing up until today – the friendship, that is, not him living with my family …

The weather was fantastic during the five weeks we were in Torquay and there were enough girls around to keep football out of our minds during our time on the coast and I can honestly say my sex-drive didn't suffer at all – it never had time to. Imagine it – a young lad from a big city who was playing at a top football club. Besides, if that failed, I always had my good looks to fall back on. That summer was also the first time I ever got drunk, thanks to Summerbee who had suggested I sample the local cider. I went out to a pub with a couple of the lads one evening and we all ordered a pint of scrumpy. I looked at the cloudy liquid in front of me and asked the barman if it was okay. He told me to look around because everyone was drinking it so I took my first gulp and to be fair, it wasn't that bad. Bobby Cunliffe and I had about five pints and believe me, five pints of scrumpy is not the done thing for a first-time drinker or even for a seasoned pro. Totally out of our heads, we left the pub with our heads full of magic and not much control over our limbs. I remember walking back to where we were based and Bob was bouncing from one wall to the other and I was crawling along walls like Spiderman. We'd missed the last bus and it was a fair walk back. The digs were at the top of this steep hill and neither of us had a hope in hell of making it, so we crouched down at the bus stop and fell asleep, happy as lambs in a barn.

We woke to the surreal sight of bright sunshine and a large queue of people waiting for the bus whilst trying to pretend we weren't really there. It was 9am and we had no time to go and get our kit so we had to jump on the next bus into town to get to the beach in time to oversee the boats. We worked that day in our underwear – like I said, real lady-killers – who could resist a skinny lad with pasty skin and a pair of Y-fronts on? I also learned of the moves City chairman had been making behind the scenes via the sports news on the radio. The whole thing had been settled, of course, by the time I became aware of developments with the upshot being that Joe Mercer had been appointed manager of the Blues. I'll confess my first reaction was: 'Oh, my God ... he's a right bastard.'

I know I was jumping to this conclusion on the strength of just one encounter the previous year, when several of the City youngsters, myself included, had gone on a course to Lileshall and Joe had been there, too. To my way of thinking, he hadn't appeared to have much time for the City lads and I felt that if he was coming to take charge at Maine Road, some of us – maybe myself included – would get the bullet. As it turned out, Joe Mercer was not the only newcomer to Maine Road, for he brought Malcolm Allison with him as his right-hand man.

Joe had had some rough experiences of his own in the managerial field and there was a time when his health suffered to such an extent many doubted he would return to the game at all. Presumably, when he was asked to become the boss of Manchester City, he thought long and hard and decided that the work load must be shared by someone who could do the coaching side of the job while Joe himself handled the overall strategy and matters in general. So he turned to Allison, the promising young Plymouth boss. It was City's good fortune because he would eventually have made it big somewhere one day, without any shadow of a doubt.

If I returned to Maine Road feeling somewhat apprehensive about the new regime, I needn't have worried. We saw a lot more of Malcolm out on the park than we did of Joe and there was never any question of our new manager having it in for the lads who had been on that course at Lilleshall. For all I know, Joe never even remembered or recognised us, but it's more likely I just got the wrong idea of him altogether. Certainly he appeared to have no preconceptions of any member of the playing staff and I found that those first impressions are not necessarily always the right ones. I learned a great deal from Joe, just as I learned a lot from Malcolm.

My first season under the new managerial team couldn't have gone much better and I went on to make 26 appearances in all competitions, scoring eight goals to boot. The side was really coming together and there was exactly the right mix of youth and experience. In one game, away to Crystal Palace, I bagged both goals in a 2-2 draw and it was the start of a run that saw me hit seven goals in six games. I played as a makeshift centre forward in some of the games for a few weeks – a plan devised by Malcolm and Joe. Like the successful 'Revie Plan' in the 1950s, this was the 'Doyle Plan' and it meant me playing as a deep-lying forward who was almost impossible to pick up. It was a simple idea but it worked a treat. I was determined to make my name at one end of the pitch – I just hadn't made my mind up which! I had my mate Glyn Pardoe to thank for covering me on my many forays forward. Glyn was an archetypal unsung hero and he was happy to remain in the shadows as I attracted headlines for hitting the back of the net.

I played one match against Blackpool with a badly injured ankle but I wouldn't come off. There were 52,661 fans crammed into Maine Road and we could all sense something special was beginning to happen and we all wanted to part of it. At the time, the chairman said:

"In the second half our hearts were in our mouths. We knew that young Doyle was in agony. He had had a bad knock and I thought we had had it. Then he got that magnificent goal! What a marvellous show he put on … in fact, what a marvellous show by the whole team."

It was good to read comments like that, especially from somebody as respected as he was. The suspected broken ankle turned out to be no more than badly bruised and I was fit for the next game away to Middlesbrough. I'd gone from earning £7 as an apprentice to £100 in barely four years and I was pinching myself it wasn't all a dream. We won the Second

Division title comfortably and things were going fantastically well. Joe and Mal wanted us to consolidate our first season back in the top division and this we did, though I made only 14 starts for the first team in the League due to the fact Stan Horne had been signed. It didn't worry me because I knew I would get my chance again and I wouldn't let my place go as easily again when I did get it back. We finished fifteenth and held our own. Things were going to plan. The next season, we would show the rest of the country what we were capable of … and how.

3

THE DYNAMIC DUO

MALCOLM ALLISON
(DAILY MAIL, 31ST JANUARY 1973)

I left Mike out of our last away game at Leicester and he wouldn't talk to me for four days. He was so bitter. He's the worst for that. But the important thing for me is that it put him back on his toes. He might not have all the quality of some but when he's on his game, he's a great competitor. When his determination is there – and it is now – he's feared by clubs all over the country.

JOE MERCER
(5TH DECEMBER 1970)

Players like Mike Doyle have explored new areas of endeavour and effort. A few players can do two jobs and there is an increasing number who can play anywhere and still express themselves and contribute. Mike does it almost automatically. He does not know how to give less than 100 per cent.

JOE MERCER and Malcolm Allison marked a turning point in the history of Manchester City. The new regime knew the first task they had to achieve was promotion from Division Two where the club could easily have become a permanent fixture had action not been taken by the board. Joe was appointed manager of the club in July 1965. The headlines at the time said he had taken on 'the toughest job in soccer' and many people would argue that not much has changed in the years since. Joe knew that the success-starved supporters wanted to see their team achieve promotion in a hurry but with style, too. His answer was: 'I want it, too … but we must build. We must make haste slowly, in the right direction. So be patient and give us time.'

I had never met Malcolm before but I recalled an incident when I went with City to watch the club play Plymouth Argyle. I was a young reserve player at the time but I was invited to become accustomed to travelling with the first team squad and to help lay the kit out. I was sat near the dugout and saw the then Plymouth boss, Malcolm Allison, and one of our coaching staff, Jimmy Meadows, start arguing. Mal was smartly dressed and Jimmy was in a tracksuit. They exchanged words and then, a moment later, Mal appeared with a bucket of water that he threw over Jimmy whilst telling him to 'fuck off.' Jimmy wasn't happy and he was a big bloke, too, but the officials stepped in to stop it escalating into a heavyweight knockout contest. You don't forget things like that so I knew Mal was going to be different in his approach and wouldn't take any shit from anyone – something I respected a great deal.

As for Joe, after a year out of the game, he had learned a lot about being patient. Football was his lifeblood but it had brought him to a state of nervous exhaustion and there were people who felt he was not making the best decision of his life when he returned to soccer by taking on the task of steering Manchester City to success. He found that there wasn't a great deal of money to spare, but the directors told him that there would be cash available provided he came up with the right player (things don't change much, do they?). His first signing turned out to be someone who gave City the best years of his playing life: Mike Summerbee.

Buzzer had been creating quite an impression playing for Swindon Town and City got him at the bargain price of £35,000 – a fee that was repaid over and over again. When Mike arrived in Manchester, the club found him accommodation at a city centre hotel. He had been in digs during his career at Swindon and I thought it would be a nice gesture if I invited him round to my home. My mum made a special Lancashire hotpot for dinner and when Mike rose from the table after almost taking the pattern off the plate, he looked at her and said: 'That's the best meal I've had in twelve months.'

Mike and I knocked around together quite a lot after that and I showed him round the town. He came to know his way as well as I did and eventually he met up with George Best. They became big mates and Mike never looked back. His career blossomed and he became an England international, as well as one of the crowd favourites at Maine Road.

But that's another story and I shall return to the subject of the management of Mercer and Allison. Their arrival heralded a new era for City and I, for one, soon sensed something special was about to happen to this famous old club. For the first time in my brief career, I felt that things were going to be different. Malcolm was the man who did most to create this impression, for he worked and almost lived with the players and he introduced revolutionary new ideas into our training sessions – in fact, for the first time in my experience, I really began to know what good coaching was all about and what a difference it could make to a team and to their game. From the moment we walked through the doors on the Monday morning, we were planning how to beat the opposition the following Saturday. Big Mal had ideas which revitalised our training routines and he was very definitely the man in charge of things out on the park. The only time we saw Joe, basically, was when he came in to give us our team talk before a game.

As a player who had made his first team debut at 17 years of age, I was still one of the new boys and I knew that I would have to keep working hard at my game to claim a regular place in the side. I had also learned more about the experienced professionals and how they felt about the game – I still hadn't forgotten that clip on the ear that Bert Trautmann had given me and the sharp words of advice he recommended I take heed of.

That wasn't the only time I incurred the wrath of a player more experienced than myself.

While I was in the reserves, I got a chasing one day from Steve Fleet although I still reckon I was right to say my piece. I walked into the dressing room one Monday morning to find Steve having a go at another player, although the player wasn't present. I had a bucket and mop in my hands – at that time I was still doing the chores – and I turned on Steve and told him it was wrong to slag players behind their backs. 'You're out of order," I said. "If you've got something to say to someone, you should say it to his face,' I told him.

Steve's reaction was swift and not entirely unexpected. 'Keep your fucking nose out," he warned and began to come after me. I dropped the bucket and mop, turned and sped out of the dressing room, down the corridor, up the tunnel, across the pitch and as far as the Platt Lane end of the ground. I waited until he had calmed down before I dared to return, but it wasn't over, not by a long chalk and as I was leaving, Fleet ran his car at me and only just missed hitting me. Next day he came up to me and said: 'I won't give you a slap, I'll just play against you.' When we came up against each other in the gym, I had to look lively, for he was giving me plenty of attention.

Finally, he caught up with me – but I managed to jump out of the way and Steve caught his foot against the wall. He limped away with a broken bone in his toe. Jimmy Meadows was standing at the other end of the gymnasium and he shouted to Steve: 'That'll teach you!' Fortunately for me, Steve saw the funny side of the whole thing after a while and we became good friends. Steve had played some first-team games and I knew he had considered I was out of line in saying my piece. Maybe he was right, but I still feel justified for saying what I said.

When Joe Mercer and Malcolm Allison took charge, I kept my place in the side and I remember the first team they chose for a game at Middlesbrough. Harry Dowd was in goal and the fullbacks were Dave Bacuzzi and Vic Gomersall. The halfback line was made up of myself, Bobby Kennedy, Alan Oakes and up front we had Mike Summerbee, Irish international Johnny Crossan, Jimmy Murray and Dave Connor, whose job it was that day to mark Davie Gibson out of the game – which he did. In fact, Connor was one of the best man-markers I've known in football and he used to get right up his quarry's back by shadowing them so effectively they either lost their rag or gave up trying to lose Dave.

The whole club had changed, in atmosphere and in attitude. Malcolm was so full of fresh ideas and his planning for the next game was meticulous, so that by the time Joe gave us our briefing before the match we already knew exactly what was what. Joe was the genial figurehead, the man who presented the public image of Manchester City. Malcolm was the man behind the scenes at that stage, driving us on in the seclusion of the training ground, giving us our cutting edge and shaping the course we had to follow.

Joe's pre-season message to us was always the same, simple, yet effective. He'd say: 'The grass is green, the paint's fresh – let's get down to work again.' He would look around the group of players, then say somewhat wistfully, I always felt: 'You lucky load of bastards. What a way to earn a living!' He was dead right, too and I'm sure he would have loved to be able to play his whole career over and over again – I know I would. I always felt that Joe was more critical of me than he was of others in the team. Why? Not because he had anything against me as a person, but because I played at wing-half – the position in which he had once excelled. I had the same sort of enthusiasm for the game that he had, but I was able to go out on the park and express that enthusiasm there, whereas his days of kicking a ball around in competitive football had ended.

Joe appreciated my enthusiasm; just as he appreciated that he could no longer play in a team himself. I think he really envied Alan Oakes and myself. Alan used to say to me: 'He's pulled me on one side again,' meaning that Joe had been having a quiet chat with Alan about his game and whenever I was in action I had the feeling that the gaffer was watching me more closely than other members of the side. After a match, he would generalise and make points about incidents which had happened, but again it seemed to me that he would always have that little bit more to say about the way I had played.

To the world at large, Joe Mercer presented a genial, avuncular figure; but his heart was still very much on the field of action and he remained wrapped up in the game and the men who played it. He could be shrewd sometimes too, when making his points. I remember the year we were going for the championship of the Second Division and we were playing against Wolves at Molineux. They were in a challenging position too, so a win was effectively worth four points (this is back when two points was all you got for a win, by the way). Wolves were beating us 2-1 and then we equalised. There were about ten minutes to go and it looked as if we would both have to be satisfied with a share of the points, when I saw an opening and went on a run that took me through Wolverhampton's defence. We were pushing up and I raced 30 yards from the back, as Johnny Crossan played a great ball over their defence.

I ran on to the through ball, just onside and took it towards goal. As the goalkeeper advanced, I hit the ball over his head and into the net. That goal gave us a 3-2 victory and naturally we were all delighted – especially me. Joe was smiling, too, but he still collared me on the coach going back to Manchester. 'You took that goal well, you young devil, but you should never have been in that position in the first place, leaving us open at the back.' It was a compliment, but a backhanded one all the same. I took his point – although I did the same thing many more times in my career and got away with it more often than not. I always enjoyed breaking through and having a crack at goal, although I realised it often left your own defenders a bit exposed, unless one of your teammates dropped back to cover for you. Mercer once said, half regretfully and half in pleasure: 'He likes attacking so much it's impossible to curb him.' So we developed a plan where Glyn Pardoe would do a covering job when he saw me moving up field.

It was on the way back from the same game at Molineux that I received a bit of a shock, for sitting on the coach was a lad whom Joe Mercer introduced to me as Stan Horne, a young wing-half from Aston Villa who Joe knew from his time as manager there. He had taken him on trial at City and Joe's eyes twinkled as he warned me: 'You'll have to pull your socks up because Stan's a wing-half too.' The boss was throwing down the gauntlet to me – maybe it was a bit of psychology on his part, or maybe he genuinely felt that Stan Horne would be a serious rival.

I never did know exactly what his motive was, but his remark about 'pulling my socks up' nettled me and I felt that he could not have been satisfied with one or other of the wing-halves he had in the side. I thought to myself: 'I'll show him how well I can play!' But we had one or two bad results and Stan claimed my place for a spell, although in the end I was the one who stayed and he moved on. There was a game at Sunderland and the Roker Park men were well below us in the table, but they beat us by the only goal of the game. Stan was in the side that afternoon and I was watching the game from the bench. Malcolm Allison was sitting next to me and at one stage I heard him muttering: 'Joe Mercer wanted Stan in the side.' At the end, as we rose, Mal tapped me on the knee and said: 'You've nothing to worry about.' I was then reinstated to the side for the rest of the season. I had no beef with Stan who was a great lad and a really dapper dresser. It was just there was no room for sentiment in football and it seemed to boil down to him or me and I was playing for my boyhood team and not about to let my dreams slip away.

There were times when you couldn't figure 'Uncle Joe' out. If ever you wanted to discuss something with him, you would find yourself walking down the tunnel and out on the pitch, with his arm around your shoulder. It used to be a standing joke that if Joe turned to the left as he walked out of the tunnel, you were in trouble, but if he turned to the right, you stood a good chance of getting a rise in pay. You might do four laps round the ground with him as you talked, but you could bet your bottom dollar that before the end conversation had turned to Barney Cresswell and Dixie Dean, two of Joe's contemporaries as players. More often than not, by the time you had finished your perambulations and got back to the dressing-room, you'd probably realise that you hadn't got around to discussing whatever you had wanted to thrash out. Maybe Joe knew that, too.

But he was always big enough to hold his hands up if he felt he'd made a mistake. A case in point concerned a lad we signed called Ralph Brand. He didn't drink, gamble or mess around with women and was a good Christian when he first arrived. Within twelve months he had been done for being drunken disorderly on two occasions, had two affairs and ended up getting divorced – that was what Manchester did to him. I recall Joe Mercer dropping me for Ralph in a game at Burnley and, during the game, Joe turned to me and apologised. "I should have played you," which I appreciated. A few throw away words, maybe, but the impact of them made me feel ten feet tall.

The partnership between Joe and Malcolm was a good one, because they were people of contrasting natures and each had something different to offer to the game. Joe was a wise old bird, experienced in every side of the game and Malcolm was the extrovert. Malcolm needed someone like Joe to lean on and yet, in a strange sort of way, he appeared to me to be the dominant figure in the partnership. Joe was the buffer on whom Mal could rely and while Mal was capable of making outrageous statements, Joe was the quiet man who played it cool, so that you got the impression he was able to keep a restraining hand on Mal when necessary and that between them they would ensure the club prospered.

Joe's notes for his pre-match team talk would be written down on a copy of The Financial Times or The Guardian and when he came into the dressing-room he would sit down and put the paper on his knee then scan through the jottings he had made. Sometimes it was hilarious, because his remarks would be spiced with real humour. And once he got the whole thing completely wrong. We were due to play Wolves and Joe came in to give us his briefing. He looked up from his notes and said to Tony Book: 'This Springbok. He has to be picked up tight, because when he's allowed to make runs down the wing he's dangerous.' We all started to look at one another, wondering what the hell Joe was on about. It was difficult for us to keep our faces straight. Then he turned to Mike Summerbee: 'You'll have to hit your crosses deep, so that they float over Banksie. We all know how good he is in the air.'

We began to realise that whatever else Joe might have to say, one thing was certain – he'd got the wrong match. He was giving us a team talk about how to play against Leicester and the 'Springbok' to whom he had been referring was the Leicester winger, Mike Stringfellow. Still nobody said anything and Joe finished his little discourse. Malcolm Allison was leaning by the door and he'd been listening to every word Joe had said. Joe never twigged that anything was wrong and as he got up from his seat Mal opened the door for him then closed it again and said to us: 'Right. I suppose you all realise that we are playing Wolves tomorrow.' And Mal took over from there. We never did discover how Joe had come to make such a mistake – we put it down to his having had a bad day on the stock market.

We played a League Cup tie against West Brom and the score finished at 3-1 for the Baggies. That was the day goalkeeper Harry Dowd gifted West Brom a goal. Harry got the ball on the edge of the 18-yard box and threw it out straight to the feet of a surprised West Brom player. He looked up, picked his spot, whacked the ball straight back from 30 yards out, curling over Harry on its way to the net. Everyone was too staggered to say anything – even the fans couldn't raise much of a cheer because it all seemed so unreal. That goal had come in the first half of the match and at the interval Joe had something to say about it. He ambled into the dressing room, looked Harry straight in the eye and said: 'I've been in this game 47 fucking years. I thought I'd seen every way in which a goal could be given away. But you just found another!'

There was a match against Cardiff, too, when Joe said his piece. Cardiff had a left-winger called Ronnie Bird and our right back, Dave Bacuzzi, just couldn't seem to get near him that afternoon. Every time Bird went down the wing, Dave would go in and 'sell' himself and be left floundering, as the winger sped away. Two crosses that were slung over from the left resulted in two goals for Cardiff and, at the end of the match, Joe Mercer was nearly frothing at the mouth as he came into the dressing room.

We saw his mouth moving into overdrive but we couldn't understand one syllable of what he was trying to say. Then we caught the final sentence: 'You sold yourself easier than a bloody prostitute ...' Joe started in again, got as far as: 'This geezer sold more dummies ...' then turned to Johnny Hart and exclaimed: 'Fucking hell, John, give me my pills!' You couldn't help but love the man and there were stories abound about him that always made you smile. Nobody was making him out to be a fool but some things were just typical of Joe and his ways.

Norah, Joe's wife always used to drop him off at Maine Road because he didn't like driving as a rule. He decided to have his own car when BMW Manchester offered him a new model for sponsorship reasons – after all, it looked good for the company to have the man in charge of the best team in the country behind the wheel of one of their cars. At that time he was living in Chorlton and he had an old wooden garage alongside his house. BMW delivered the car to his house and left him with keys. Joe had a look and discovered it was an automatic – something he'd never driven before. He turned the engine on, shifted it into gear, took the handbrake off and sped backwards through the wooden garage, demolishing it completely! He'd done ten yards in it and ruined the car and the garage – like I said, only Joe ...

Yet he was the genial guy who attended functions and projected the right image for the club. This didn't mean he hadn't a great deal of knowledge about the game, but he recognised that Malcolm Allison was there to do the grafting with the players on the park and he left Mal in charge of that department. Under Joe Mercer's reign, City came out of the Second Division as champions, claimed the Championship of the First Division, the FA Cup, the League Cup, the European Cup-Winners Cup and four Charity Shields. At that point, no other club in the country had won so many trophies in such a short space of time. The heading on the club notepaper said 'Manager – Joe Mercer' and he was the man at the top, the one with whom people associated the club's success, although he always ensured that Malcolm Allison got due credit for the work he had put in.

I always felt at that time that Mal was so wrapped up in the players that so long as we were winning things, nothing else really affected him. If people outside Maine Road had the impression that City's success was a one-man effort, it was wrong and it was not fair. Yet, having said that, I must also say that Mal did get plenty of publicity – most of it self-generated – and there was no question that the players gave him all the credit he deserved and at least he had the satisfaction of knowing this. Today, people recognise both men were equally responsible for the success they achieved and it's fair to say that alone, they wouldn't have achieved what they did at Maine Road – a fact borne out by both men's records in the past.

I had a lot of admiration for Mal for what he had done for the club and I know many of the players felt the same as I did. He changed the playing methods and in this respect it was Malcolm Allison who put City on the map. He was an extrovert, a flamboyant character and there was no one else in the game to touch him. He gave Manchester City an aura of glamour and while some people may have thought he carried things to excess at times, the players didn't look at it in that light. They judged Malcolm Allison by the results the team had achieved – and we had done so many great things together.

Perhaps we were also so wrapped up in the football side that we didn't see what was beginning to happen off the field. Even today I cannot say that I consciously realised the parting of the ways was near for Joe and Mal. All I have to go on is what I read in the papers at the time. Suddenly it seemed that the partnership was starting to split at the seams. Malcolm wanted to be team manager in name, to get public acknowledgement of the work he had done behind the scenes. In the end, the parting came quite swiftly and Joe Mercer left after being shabbily treated in view of what he had done for the club. He wasn't happy with the new role he'd been given and joined Coventry City in a general manager role. Allison was officially handed the job of managing the players at Maine Road and that was that. Well, not quite, because there were some storms ahead and I was a central figure in one of the numerous dust-ups which occurred during his regime.

4

WHEN WE WERE KINGS

MIKE DOYLE

If I had to pack the game in tomorrow I would go straight out and buy a season ticket for Maine Road. And I would be there at the reserve, youth team and bounce games. I grew up in a town that only wanted to know Manchester United and I've been lucky enough to help change that.

I KNOW YOU'VE probably heard this story before or know of the history of how City became the champions of England. But seeing as it was the last time the Blues won what is today known as the Premiership, I think it is worth retelling in detail, if for no other reason than to prove to those of you who were either too young or not around that the Blues were once undisputed heavyweight champions of England and Europe. I hope I'm wrong, but with the rich getting richer in football all the time, you wonder if City will take the title again in the near future. It is possible and things are improving in leaps and bounds so maybe I'm being a little sceptical – but then again, I am a City fan and it comes with the territory.

So let's go back to the run-in of the 1967/68 season and indulge in what still is the most glorious time in the club's history. As the contenders for the championship that year entered the final straight, Leeds were up there in contention, along with City, Manchester United and Liverpool. The final league table shows that City finished top, with 58 points and that United were the runners-up, two points adrift, while Liverpool claimed third place three points behind. That season was a tense battle which went right to the final 90 minutes, by

48

which time only two clubs – City and United – remained as the real rivals ... and the destination of the title was settled both at Old Trafford and at St James's Park.

Nine matches from the finishing post it was still a four-horse race and at that stage the smart money was on Leeds who were leading the pack, although in City and United's case, it was only on goal average, while Liverpool were two points behind, but with a game in hand. Three teams had taken 45 points from their 33 matches. So the matches came and went and, at the death, Leeds United and Liverpool were out of the hunt for the title. The battle was going to be between City and United. Yet it was not all plain sailing for us, because we hit a bit of a rocky patch around March. There came a week when we had no fixture because there was a FA Cup tie involving the team we should have played, so we all went to Blackpool for the weekend.

This was just before the hectic Easter programme and everyone was feeling jaded and tired; the pressures of battling for supremacy in the title race had begun to show. It was an inspired decision to take us there and when we arrived at our hotel, Malcolm said to us: 'Right, forget about football, just enjoy yourselves.' And we did. During the day, we played golf and in the evenings we relaxed and had a few drinks. I say 'a few drinks', but in fact we really sank some ale and I reckon that must be the first and possibly the only time that a team has wound itself up by going out on a bender.

By the time we were leaving, we were also leaving all the tension behind us. We felt in good fettle and we were raring to go. They say a change is as good as a rest and that break at breezy, bracing Blackpool had washed the cobwebs from our brains and renewed our appetite for the battle ahead. It was perfectly timed and we started to get the right results again.

We came to the final run-in with two matches left to play and the championship in our sights. The penultimate game

49

was against Tottenham Hotspur, at White Hart Lane. We had always done well against Spurs at Maine Road, but we knew that we needed to pick up both points in London – and White Hart Lane hadn't been one of our favourite grounds in recent years. Spurs were up for the game and they had a damned good side. Martin Chivers, a big powerful striker, was then at his peak and there was also their famous old warhorse Dave Mackay to contend with in the middle of the park, while Jimmy Greaves was still banging the goals in for fun. It was just the sort of match you don't want at such a crucial stage but at least we could go there knowing the City fans would be there in force to cheer us on. We knew exactly what we had to do and that was go for the throat and try and hit them so hard they wouldn't be able to recover. We set our stall out to win that game, in the quickest possible time.

For the first half-hour, we virtually played Tottenham off the park and Colin Bell gave one of the finest displays I have ever seen and that's saying something considering his consistently high standards. In those first 30 minutes, I don't think Spurs had one single shot. We were going at it hell-for-leather and every City player seemed to be giving two hundred percent effort with full-blooded tackling, inch-perfect passing and ruthless finishing. We'd given the North London outfit a real hammering, we were three up and coasting towards victory by the time the interval arrived. But, like a distance runner that hits the front too soon, the pace we had set for ourselves had been too great during the first 45 minutes and, as the second half wore on, we began to tire dramatically. We simply couldn't keep the pressure up and by the time the last half-hour loomed, it was obvious that we had pretty much burned ourselves out. Spurs started to build up their a head of steam, sensing that they were still in with a chance of snatching something from the game and Chivers rapped in a couple of shots which hit the woodwork. Things were starting to happen – at the wrong end of the pitch, so far as we were concerned.

They went on the attack again and a cross curled over from the right. Alan Oakes and I went up for the ball and he shouted 'My ball!' so I left it to him. Suddenly, out of nowhere, a hand appeared and pushed the ball away – Alan and myself both thought at that moment it was our goalkeeper, Ken Mulhearn, doing his stuff, but it wasn't ... that hand belonged to our centre-half, George Heslop and Spurs were awarded a penalty. They scored and pegged us back to 3-1. For the final 20 minutes, Tottenham put us under fantastic pressure and they could so easily have got a draw if they'd have taken the chances presented to them but, as it turned out, that was the end of the scoring and as we trudged into the dressing room our chests were heaving – partly from our all-out exertions and not least of all from sighs of relief. We'd sweated blood and tears to ensure we didn't throw the title away. Joe Mercer came in and while he was delighted at the final result, he nearly went spare over that penalty goal we had conceded.

He rounded on poor George Heslop. 'You had two men standing behind you and the ball ... and yet you knock it away with your hand!' exploded Joe. But George always had a ready answer and he was quick to explain away what had happened. 'I wasn't going to go for it,' he said, 'and then I decided to go for it after all and as I was in the air, Jimmy Greaves caught me on the funny bone and my hand just flashed out and flicked the ball!'

We all started to laugh and Joe Mercer just wiped his brow. "You're a fucking liar, George, but we've won ... we've won.' Despite our tiredness as we had trooped off the field, 30 minutes after the final game we had recovered all our bounce – in fact, we were wishing that we could get at Newcastle United, our final opponents, there and then and if we'd been able to do so, I think we would have murdered them. That was the mood we were in.

But we had to contain ourselves and wait for the chance to become champions. Training was fantastic all week and we all felt on top of the world. To us, it was a matter of doing what we had done all season for one more game. If we did, we were guaranteed the championship. The only team that could catch us was Manchester United and you can imagine how that fired us up even more. They were playing Sunderland at Old Trafford and since Sunderland had nothing to play for, a lot of people reckoned that our journey to St James' Park would end in misery. United were rated as stone-cold certainties to beat Sunderland and many people thought we would struggle to get two points at Newcastle, who gave nothing away on their own ground. Not surprisingly, when the day came, half the football fans in Manchester were trying to claim vantage points at Old Trafford, while the other half were making the long trek up the Al to St James's Park.

The build-up to the two matches during the week had been tremendous. We felt as if we were going to play for the world club championship or in a European Cup final. It was such an electric atmosphere that it was difficult to realise that this final match, the decider, was 'just' a League game. I didn't feel there was any way we were going to lose out at Newcastle and the mood of confidence was shared by my team-mates. Indeed, we were not just super-confident … we were almost arrogant in our conviction that the championship was coming back to Maine Road but perhaps a touch of arrogance is the stuff champs are made of. There were plenty of Newcastle supporters around when we arrived at our hotel and I think even they were soon of the opinion that we were going to beat their team the next afternoon.

Saturday morning was the first time that signs of tension began to show. This was D-day and it seemed that no one was doing the things they usually did on the morning before a match. We had an early lunch and got down to the pre-match briefing.

Both Joe Mercer and Malcolm Allison spoke with one voice and they were explicit: 'It's all been said. You know what you have to do – so go and do it. Win today and you're the champions.' They kept it simple and had said all that needed to be said.

Normally, when you get to the opposition's ground, you go out and take a look at the pitch but, on this occasion, very few of our players made the customary inspection. It was as if we all wanted to dispense with the preliminaries and get straight into the game. Wherever you looked around St James's Park, there was a sea of blue-and-white scarves and I'm still convinced that half the Newcastle supporters that day were waving scarves in the City colours, because – despite their loyalty to their own team – they really felt we deserved to take the championship and they wanted us to win it.

When the game finally began, it was a thrill-a-minute roller coaster ride and, looking back now, it still seems the most incredible game I ever played in. Inside the first ten minutes, we were a goal ahead. I collected the ball from Colin Bell and, out of the corner of my eye, I saw Mike Summerbee at the near post. I was outside the box and I'd decided to have a crack at goal myself but, when I saw Mike, I changed my mind and aimed the ball for the post. Franny Lee was there too, just behind Mike, waiting for anything that was going, but the ball went straight to Buzzer. He made just a yard of ground, then clipped the ball over the 'keeper's body and into the net. It was the kind of start we had dreamed of … but Newcastle kicked off again and went straight down to our end of the pitch and equalised.

Big George Heslop was normally one of the coolest customers you could meet, but this time he got himself into a tangle. He got possession of the ball in the middle of the park and could have pushed it around to almost anyone he chose; instead he held on to the ball for so long that he was robbed. Newcastle broke away down the left then and 'Pop' Robson, never a player to waste half a chance, stuck the ball into the City net. So we were back to square one and still had it all to do.

With half an hour of the game gone, though, the hordes of City supporters were yelling and cheering as we took the lead again. It was Neil Young who scored – a fabulous goal it was, too. Alan Oakes played a the ball up to Youngy and he controlled it at waist height, still with his back to goal and after cushioning the ball with his body, he turned and struck a shot on the half-volley from more than 20 yards. I'll swear the ball never travelled more than four feet above the grass and it zipped through the air like a bullet, finishing in the net before the Newcastle 'keeper could even move.

But ten minutes before half-time, we had lost the lead again and George Heslop became convinced that it wasn't his day at all. He had been robbed of the ball by Jackie Sinclair when Newcastle scored their first goal and this time it was Wyn Davies who took the ball off George, giving Sinclair the chance to go straight through the middle and hit a tremendous goal from just outside the box. Suddenly, and for the first time, we began to think that we could even lose this game because we just couldn't create a bit of breathing space. It was clear that the Newcastle players wanted a victory every bit as much as we did. We were playing for the Championship … but their pride was at stake and they were letting us know it.

It wasn't the time for recriminations, as we sat in the dressing room. The score was 2-2, so we had to go out and start all over again. The adrenaline began to flow once more and, for the first ten minutes of the second half, we were very composed, allowing Newcastle no rope at all. We wore them down in that opening spell of the half, much as we had done at Tottenham the week before, and cracked their defence with another goal from Neil Young. He struck the ball with so much power from the left-hand side of the box that his angled shot whizzed past the full-back and the goalkeeper, to make the score 3-2.

Ten minutes later, we hand one hand on the championship trophy. Franny Lee collected a great pass through the middle, skipped past two players and, as the 'keeper advanced from goal he clipped it past him to put us 4-2 ahead. I leapt delightedly in the air and grabbed the nearest team-mate, Tony Book. At least, I thought it was Tony – until I found I was clutching the referee in a bear hug. He took one look at me and said: 'Do it again and I'll book you.' Who ever said referees had to have a humour by-pass to progress? Probably me, I suppose.

Fifteen minutes to go and we were coasting towards the title … five minutes to go and all hell was let loose again. Newcastle got the ball down the right and caught us out at the back. Sinclair sped down the wing, crossed the ball to Newcastle's big centre-half, John McNamee and he nodded it home. After that, we had our backs to the wall, as United went flat out for an equaliser and you can believe me when I say that I was willing the referee to blow his whistle and signal the end of the match. Somehow, we held out, despite the frenzied efforts of the home team to finish all-square and when the referee blew his whistle for full-time, it was the sweetest sound I think I had ever heard. It was over and we knew we were at last champions of England.

What we didn't know – although it didn't matter, anyway – was how Manchester United had fared at Old Trafford. No one had told us how they were going on at half-time, so it wasn't until we reached the dressing-room that we learned they had lost 2-1 against Sunderland. That made us clear-cut champions and no one could dispute our right to the crown. It was bedlam, of course. The City supporters had invaded the pitch at the end of the game and almost engulfed us and there were people coming in and out of the dressing room to offer their congratulations … but Glyn Pardoe and I just sat there and shed tears.

It was that kind of an emotional occasion, Glyn and I had been at the club ever since we were kids and to us, winning the League was the ultimate. Naturally, the champagne was soon flowing, but I was too excited to savour fully the sweet taste of success. However, we had to get bathed and changed and make our way back to Manchester down the A1, so we had plenty to do. That journey will live in my mind as long for as I live, because our team coach was just one of a cavalcade of coaches and cars, all decked out in sky blue.

The queue of traffic was so great that progress was slow and we had to keep stopping, bumper to tail. I remember Malcolm Allison leaping down from the coach on more than one occasion and running around to the cars which were keeping us company. He was brandishing a bottle of champagne and inviting the fans to have a drink and share in our triumphant homecoming. I don't remember giving much thought to Old Trafford and the scenes of dejection there must have been in the Manchester United dressing-room when news of our famous victory came through. United's defeat was academic, in any case, because we had won. No one could take the championship away from us and that day was undoubtedly the greatest moment of my footballing career.

5

THE BLUES GO MARCHING ON (AND ON)

MIKE DOYLE

(THE SUN, 22ND MARCH 1999)

*They might have had Best, Charlton and Law but when we played
them it was a piece of piss. City would win 4-0 or 5-1 every time.*

WINNING THE FA Cup is something special for the players and
the fans of the successful club. Tony Book was our skipper when
we won the trophy in the spring of 1969. The FA Cup trail began
for us that season at St James's Park, Newcastle and it sticks in
my mind that Ian Niven, who was then a City director, was
forecasting at the start that we would win the trophy. We got a 0-
0 draw at Newcastle and finished the job off at Maine Road,
beating Newcastle 2-0. I think somewhere close to 120,000 fans
watched the two games overall.

By the time we had got through to the quarter-finals,
Tottenham Hotspur were all that stood between us and a place
in the semi-finals. That match still counts as the hardest of the
lot. In previous encounters we had always given Spurs a good
going-over and they seemed to be afraid of us; but when they
came to Maine Road for that Cup tie their attitude was different
from anything we had ever known.

Spurs came with a definite game-plan and set out from the
start to chase and harry us and I began to wonder if our run
was going to come to a disappointing end. It looked odds on
them at least taking us back to White Hart Lane for a replay ...
until, with something like ten minutes to go, Franny Lee
turned a half-chance into a goal. Pat Jennings got a hand to it,
but he couldn't stop it or us progressing into the semi-finals.

That brought us up against Everton and they seemed to be everyone's favourites to win the Cup that season. So when we went out at Villa Park, there was no doubt about it, we were the underdogs and they had already beaten us twice that season in the league. They had that famous midfield line of Ball, Harvey and Kendall and so we had to do something special to counteract the influence they could have on the game. Malcolm Allison spelled it out that we had to keep these three quiet and we marked them so well that they scarcely got a kick in the middle of the park, giving us a chance to play a bit ourselves.

We just wore Everton down and restricted their midfield three all the way along the line. I could see that Bally was getting sicker and sicker by the minute and Everton's big centre-forward, Joe Royle, wasn't able to get any sort of service on the day. In the second half, we won a corner and I went up field for it. The ball came over and I headed it, aiming for Mike Summerbee. He pushed the ball on to Tommy Booth, who smacked it into the Everton net.

That left just a few minutes to go and we made no mistake about holding on to our lead. As soon as we got into the dressing-room, I could tell from the attitude of my team-mates that we were going to win the FA Cup. If we could beat Everton, no one could stop us – and we didn't consider Leicester, our opponents in the final, to be any great shakes.

It was my first visit to Wembley and I was thrilled. It was real Boy's Own stuff and the dream of any youngster to have the chance to hold that famous old trophy aloft. We prepared for the final at Weybridge, in Surrey and the training was very light-hearted. There was almost a carnival atmosphere about the City camp, as if we knew that once the formalities had been completed, all would be right on the day. We enjoyed ourselves on the golf course by the hotel and everything was nice and relaxed. We went to the cinema, dropped in for a drink at the pub across the road and generally just chilled out. Joe and Malcolm knew exactly how to prepare us for the big occasion and this is an often overlooked part of their management. We were not put on a ball and chain and we responded accordingly. No one talked about the possibility of us beating Leicester ... it was a case of 'when', not 'if', we won. I didn't get butterflies until we were driving down Wembley Way. When I saw all the people milling around and the twin towers of Wembley in the distance, it hit me like a sledgehammer between the eyes. In 90 minutes' time, all these people would be inside the stadium – and we would be going out on the pitch to do battle with Leicester. That drive down Wembley Way remains one of the best memories of my career. But I was disappointed with the dressing rooms – ours seemed to be high up and all the players seemed to be bunched together, as if we were in a confined space, not unlike the changing rooms a thousand Sunday League teams use week in, week out and not what you expected at one of the world's premier arenas. I became accustomed to that dressing-room after that day, for on two more Cup occasions – against West Brom and Newcastle, in the League Cup – City occupied the 'home' dressing-room.

Another disappointment was the turf, which was bare and bumpy. My experience of it up to then had been confined to viewing it on television and I had expected it to be like a billiard table. I hoped it wouldn't upset the way we played, because we liked to push the ball around. I was getting all kinds of nervous thoughts while we were out inspecting the pitch. Then we walked back down the tunnel, to get changed for the game.

Everything changed as we lined up and walked up the tunnel yet again – this time to .get down to the real business of playing a football match and winning another trophy for our fans to boast about. It was a fabulous experience. You walked slightly uphill and as you came to the mouth of the tunnel you could see the people at the top of the stand … then, as you emerged, the whole place erupted in a crescendo of sound. We lined up on the pitch for the presentation and I shook hands with Princess Anne. I can remember thinking that she was very attractive and different in the flesh than she looked in the newspapers and on television.

Then she moved on and it had to be Tony Coleman who capped the lot. As skipper Tony Book introduced him, Princess Anne said: 'I'm pleased to meet you' … and TC came straight back: 'Give my regards to your Mum and Dad. Tell them to come to the reception afterwards.'

It was typical of TC to think of something like that to say, in his rich Scouse accent, when the rest of us were fumbling for words and wishing we could get started on the game. I never did find out whether or not someone was having a joke, but at our victory banquet afterwards there was a telegram which read something like this: 'Sorry we couldn't make it. Otherwise engaged, yours sincerely, Elizabeth.' I've wondered ever since if Princess Anne really did tell her parents about the invitation Tony Coleman had extended.

As for the game, Leicester gave us quite a bit of trouble during the first ten minutes – in fact, they surprised us – but then we began to make our all-round power tell and we started getting a grip on things. There was only one goal in the game, but we could have won by two or three and no one would have argued. Neil Young got the goal that settled it, after play had been going for half an hour. There was a good build-up on the right; Mike Summerbee took on David Nish and held him off by sheer strength, then laid the ball to Youngy. He hit a thunderous drive with his left foot, from just inside the edge of the box and Peter Shilton had no chance.

Leicester had passed up two chances – one a great opening from Peter Rodrigues, the other when Harry Dowd made a tremendous save from Allan Clarke – but once we had struck, I just couldn't see them scoring and fortunately, they didn't.

It had been my job to organise the defensive wall during the game and I used to stand on the end facing Harry Dowd to ensure he was happy with the cover in front of him. As I turned around, Leicester took the free kick and the ball hit me straight in the bollocks. "Fuckin' hell!" I screamed and collapsed on the ground in agony – is there any there anything worse, especially with 100,000 fans pissing their sides and millions more watching on television doing the same thing?

The next day, back in Manchester, we went to the Town Hall and met all the dignitaries and after a reception with the fans – there must have been 250,000 outside the town hall – I went home to my parents' house. My dad embraced me and congratulated me on our success at Wembley but my mum looked annoyed. "We never brought you up to use language like that, Michael," she said, pulling me down a peg or two. I hadn't counted on her lip-reading and I was careful not to curse again when the cameras were on me.

One of the important things which came out of that victory was that we were beginning to realise just what a good team we really were. We had won the League Championship the previous year; now we had collected the FA Cup and we felt we could achieve even more. That was the feeling among the players and it was crystallised by Colin Bell when he predicted that we'd win the League Cup the following season. He was a good prophet, but he wasn't one hundred percent correct. We went on to win not only the League Cup, but the European Cup-Winners Cup as well, so that in three years we could claim to have captured four major trophies and with all due respect to Liverpool's achievements in Europe and the League during the 1970s, I'd like to remind people what seems to have been forgotten … that City became the first English club to win a European trophy, as well as a major domestic prize, in the one season.

The spring of 1970 saw City on the threshold of this unique double and to add spice to the occasion, in the League Cup Manchester United were our semi-final opponents. It was a two-legged tie and the first game was played at Maine Road, so we knew it was down to us to win – and win well – on our own ground. Old Trafford would be like a cauldron for the return match and we could expect no favours when United got us there.

In the City dressing room before the game, we were all feeling tense. The importance of the next 90 minutes had got through to us but we were given a great boost when Colin Bell scored a first-half goal and at half-time we felt that we could double that tally before the 90 minutes were up. United had fought their way back into the match during the ten minutes before the break, though and when the second half began we suddenly seemed to freeze. While we were still trying to put our game together again, Bobby Charlton broke through and scored a tremendous goal. He ran the ball into the 18-yard box and whacked it home from around eight yards. That goal rocked us on our heels.

But it also made us more determined than ever to get the better of our greatest rivals and we began to play again ourselves. Our chance came when Franny Lee had the ball laid up to him inside the box and he turned centre-half Ian Ure. The big blond Scot, who had joined United from Arsenal, couldn't compete with Franny's pace and he brought him down. Franny stepped up to take the spot kick to make it 2-1 which ended up being the final score. The penalty was fully justified, even if our second goal had come slightly against the run of play. We were facing a real battle for the return leg at Old Trafford but we had turned them over a few times recently and knew that if we played as well as we could, we'd be at Wembley again.

United had done nothing for a few years, while City were on the march and they had become a bit desperate to turn the tide, even though they were still commanding massive gates, so the atmosphere at Old Trafford was almost at fever pitch. There was an air of tingling expectancy, as the teams went out on the park. We soon struck form and United keeper Alex Stepney couldn't do a thing about the goal we scored. Two or three shots had been blocked in the United goalmouth area and then Alex stopped another effort, but Ian Bowyer was on hand to tap the ball into the net.

Our lead didn't last long, though, because United scored about five minutes afterwards, when they made their first real attack. Paul Edwards went through from a defensive position and hit a great goal into the top corner of the net. We led 3-2, on aggregate with the second half still to come.

That was when George Best picked the ball up about 35 yards from goal, wriggled his way through the City defence and hit a shot which Joe Corrigan first grasped, then let drop. Denis Law didn't miss chances like those and he struck the ball into the net, bringing the aggregate score level. Yet we were still playing well and, although United had equalised, when I looked at the faces of their players it seemed to me that they still felt under pressure. They should have been registering real delight and oozing confidence ... but I sensed that they weren't able to believe in themselves, even then.

We built up another attack and a free kick was awarded against United, just outside the 18-yard box. It was an indirect free kick and, as they lined up their defensive wall, the referee still had his arm pointing skywards. When Franny Lee ran forward to take the kick, we all knew he was going to shoot – and to this day I don't think he could explain why he hammered in a direct shot, when the kick was an indirect award. But hit the ball he did ... and Alex Stepney tried to save it. He could have stood and let the ball go into the net and it wouldn't have counted but, instead, he did his best to stop the shot and Mike Summerbee raced in to put the ball past him.

Naturally, Alex took some stick over that goal. But since that match, I've spoken to a lot of goalkeepers about the incident and they all agree that when you see the ball coming at you it's an instinctive reaction to try to stop it. Especially when it comes from behind a wall of defenders for, though it may be an indirect free kick, there's always the danger of a deflection. I still think Alex did the right thing.

There were no more goals and that Summerbee goal meant that we'd won the tie 4-3 over the two matches and, after the game, I could see how dejected Bobby Charlton and Denis Law were. It would have meant so much for them and United to return to Wembley and have a shout, after several barren years. They knew the club needed to do something tangible, in terms of reaching a final or even winning a trophy, to put United back on the map. But we didn't spare any sympathy for the losers. For us, that semi-final victory confirmed our right to be called top dogs. We gloated ... and if we had had salt, we would have gladly rubbed it into United's wounds. That's how it was and still is and besides, I enjoyed it.

My memories of the final against West Brom will always be linked with a trip to Portugal, where we had to play Academica Coimbra in the first leg of the European Cup-Winners Cup quarter-finals. Coimbra were being dismissed as a side composed of students, whose main aim in life was to pass their exams. Football, it was suggested, came very much second to studies and City shouldn't have any trouble at all. Everyone seemed to be playing this theme and I'm afraid we began to swallow the talk that Coimbra were there for the taking. We allowed ourselves to be lulled into a false sense of security.

It took us only ten minutes' play to realise what we were up against. Coimbra had some hatchet men and their all-black strip seemed to give them a sinister appearance. At first, we were more concerned with keeping out of trouble and being one hundred percent ready for the League Cup final against

At Maine Road for the last-ever fixture against Southampton in May 2003.

The all-conquering Reddish Vale school team. I'm in the middle sharing a ball with Tony Dove.

That's me (far left, looking smart) and the Stockport Boys squad. I was out of the side with a broken ankle.

Me as a 16-year old apprentice professional.

A jog with the other apprentices at Maine Road.

City youth team, 1963.

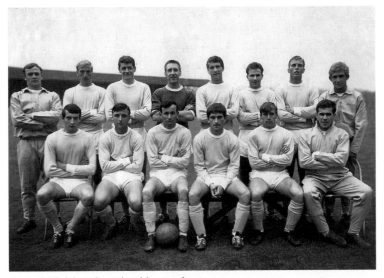

Second Division championship squad.

George Poyser and a few of the lads promoting a new football - neither
George nor the football lasted very long.

In action for the Blues in 1968.

My debut for the England U-23s v Hungary at Goodison Park, 1968.

The championship-winning squad 1968.

A celebratory pint after winning the championship at the Fletcher's Arms, Denton, with Ian Niven, godfather to my daughter Natalie, behind the bar.

My wedding to Cheryl in 1969 with Glyn Pardoe, Joe Mercer and Tottenham's Phil Beal.

Booked with West Brom's Jeff Astle after five minutes of the League Cup Final in 1970.

Celebrating with the City fans after victory.

I scored a few against Nottingham Forest. This one was at Maine Road in 1970.

Hitting the woodwork against Spurs at Maine Road.

Stan Gibson helps me celebrate my Player of the Year award - what a top man Stan was and is much missed by everyone at City.

Another booking - this time against Crystal Palace in January 1971.

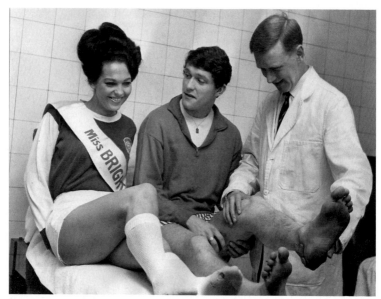

Miss Brighton, on a whistle-stop tour of the UK, pops in for a bit of physio with Peter Blakey.

Thumbs up in the bath, 1971. I'd been asked what I thought of Miss Brighton!

Exchanging words with Emlyn Hughes and Tommy Smith at Anfield in
August 1972. Emlyn was whining as usual.

'He's cuffed me!' Leighton James is about to bleat to the referee against
Burnley at Turf Moor in October 1973. We lost 0-3.

My penalty miss against Arsenal in March 1973 - no other fucker would take it!

Making up for it with a goal from closer range against Spurs.

'Fucking hell, Joe!' – the picture says it all.

Me? Disagreeing with a referee? Never! (v Leeds United 1974).

Challenging Billy Bremner with Tommy Booth and Tony Towers looking on.

1973/74 City squad.

West Brom the following Saturday but, when we saw the way it was, we began to get stuck in ourselves. With half-time looming, we could see that Coimbra were beginning to tire a bit, although in Nene they had a player who still looked as if he might do some damage to our chances. Fortunately, he limped off early in the second half and we were thankful to see the back of him. We stuck grimly to our task and settled for containing Coimbra, in the confident belief that when we got them back to Maine Road we would be able to call the tune. We held firm to leave Portugal with a 0-0 draw and that was enough for us, as we climbed aboard the aircraft which was to take us back to England. But our problems hadn't ended, for we were diverted to Birmingham and a three-hour coach ride on to London wasn't exactly the best way to start getting ready for a Cup final – but no one cared … we were laughing and joking, despite our tiredness. All we wanted to do was to play the game against West Brom.

Once again, I was disappointed in the Wembley pitch, which, unbelievably, had been ploughed up by horses. I was even more gutted when West Brom scored. A cross came over and, though Joe Corrigan came out, he didn't get to the ball. Jeff Astle was there and headed it almost through Joe's hands. We kept creating chances, but we weren't looking as if we would score and half-time came with the Baggies still 1-0 ahead. In the dressing-room, Malcolm Allison reminded us: 'Come on … you're halfway to winning a European trophy … get out there and win this one and you'll make it that much easier for yourselves in Europe.'

In the second half, we began to overpower West Brom. Possibly we had suffered in the first half from a reaction after all the travelling we had done and the game we had played in Portugal in midweek, but we really geared up for the final 45 minutes. Mike Summerbee was hampered by an injury, but he managed to get the ball and play it on to Colin Bell, who in turn flicked it across goal. I raced in on the blind side of the defenders and from close on a dozen yards out I sent in a shot that flew into the net. Even though the game went to extra time, we knew then that it was just a matter of time. We were going to win.

Asa Hartford was still a West Brom player then and he had gone off. He was whacked and his team-mates looked as if they were the ones who had been involved in a midweek European tie and had flown a couple of thousand miles around Europe. I'd had the job of marking Asa and I think he would ruefully admit that I did a pretty effective job that day. In the second half of extra time, we cracked West Brom's resistance. Glyn Pardoe, not famed for his goal-poaching ability bundled the ball home for the winner and that was it, there was no way back for the Baggies and it was especially sweet for me and Glyn, being such good mates, to have scored a goal each at Wembley and it's something to tell our grandson in years to come. So we had followed up the title and the FA Cup successes by collecting the League Cup ... and there was still the Cup-Winners Cup to come.

Lifted by our League Cup triumph, it was all systems go when we got the chance to have another crack at Coimbra, this time on our own ground and in front of our own supporters. I'll say this for Coimbra – at Maine Road they kicked us four times harder than they had done in Portugal and it was the first time I had ever come across a massed-defensive system which had all eleven men back. They were cynical and so blatant were their defensive tactics, it seemed all the more ridiculous that only three weeks earlier people had been dismissing them as a bunch of students whose main interest was in sitting for their degrees. They all had degrees, all right – in how to mix it out on the pitch.

It looked like being a frustrating night for us because something like 80 minutes had gone by and there were still no goals. Then Tony Towers struck. The ball bobbled off one of their defenders and Tony hit it first time. It was scrappy but it did the trick and it seemed the only way we could have got a goal, the way the tie had been panning out. We won 1-0 and went through to the semi-finals. There we came up against Schalke 04 and though we lost 1-0 away, we scored five goals to one in the return. I hit the first, inside ten minutes and it was a good time for us to score. That made it 1-1 on aggregate and we still had 80 minutes to do the rest. We murdered them.

The final took place in Vienna and we were up against the Poles of Gornik and their fans apparently had not been allowed visas to travel, with the result that the crowd looked as if it might have been watching a Third or Fourth Division game. I think the gate was only about 10,000 and they were mostly City supporters who had had to go a long way to support their team. A two-legged final at both grounds would have been far better and allowed all the fans to have seen us in action rather than the hardy collection who made it on the night. And it rained … how it rained! The giant Praeter Stadium was swept by torrents of rain and the pitch became almost a quagmire.

We went into a 1-0 lead when Neil Young was put through on the left-hand side of the park. He took the ball on, drew the keeper and waltzed round him, only to be brought down by a desperate defender. The redoubtable Franny Lee made no mistake from the penalty spot to give us the advantage but, after about 20 minutes, I ceased to take any further part in the proceedings because of an ankle injury. An opponent went over the top, from behind and I copped the lot. Dave Ewing carried me off, humping me over his shoulders like a sack of coal and as I left the field in this undignified manner, I heard Malcolm Allison calling at me: 'Get back on, you big girl! You're getting soft!'

I gave him a right mouthful back and when Mal came down to

get a good look at the ankle he knew the pain was real enough. I'd strained an Achilles tendon and the ankle had to be put in plaster. So Ian Bowyer went on in my place and it wasn't long before we scored another goal, with Neil Young the marksman. Gornik could never really fathom us out and although they got a goal near the end, there was never any doubt as to which side was going to collect the trophy. We celebrated in style at our hotel after the match and, although I couldn't do much except sit around and have a few drinks, Franny Lee and Mike Summerbee showered each other with champagne and Big Mal stood on the piano, singing his head off.

We played Gornik again the following season in the same trophy. We'd made it to the quarter-final and we travelled to Katowice to play the first leg. We landed at Krakow, where there had been a concentration camp during the war. There was plenty of snow there – I don't think I've ever seen as much in my life. As we embarked on the coach for the long trip to our headquarters, we were fascinated by the horse-drawn sledges which were clearly a part of the everyday winter scene there. We didn't expect that the game would ever get under way, because the conditions really were arctic. Gornik had been taking a winter break of their own, for they had spent the best part of a fortnight in Spain, where the sun was shining and they had done pretty much all their match preparations while they were abroad. They badly wanted to beat us, too, after their defeat the previous year in Vienna.

On the day of the game, the pitch was cleared of snow and it resembled a skating rink and felt like one, too. I maintain to this day that we should have worn blades instead of studs. There were 100,000 people packed into the stadium and they gave their heroes every encouragement – even before the kick-off. When the signal came for us to leave the dressing room, we found ourselves face to face with the Gornik lads ... and discovered that they were all wearing nylon tights. As we stood in this big marble hall, just before walking out on the pitch side by side, Franny Lee cuddled up to one of the Gornik players and stroked the nylon on his legs. Then, with a cheeky grin on his face, Franny asked: 'Do you wear suspenders, too?'

It was good for a laugh and it helped to remove the tension we were feeling, but it was no joke for us when the Poles got us out on the park. They gave us a real roasting. In fact, they murdered us. They had a fellow called Lubianski and he was one of the best footballers I've ever seen. He played up front for Gornik and he scored their first goal out of nothing. He hit the woodwork twice and soon the Poles were two goals ahead. There seemed to be absolutely nothing we could do to stem the tide and the way things were going I could see us losing by four or five clear goals.

In the second half, we began to get a bit more into the game, but this fellow Lubianski still gave us cause for the shivers. For the third time in the match he hit the woodwork and once more we were praying that our luck would hold and that we would get away with nothing more than a 2-0 defeat and a moral hiding. We held out grimly until the final whistle went and we were released from the torment. The Polish fans erupted as they cheered the Gornik men and we stood around feeling a bit disconsolate for a few seconds.

Franny Lee and Mike Summerbee who had been the only two players we could get into the Gornik half of the field, suddenly got together and started leaping up and down like dervishes. The Polish players had obviously been delighted by their victory – you could see the elation on their faces – but when they saw these two City players jumping around as if we had won, the Gornik men's expressions began to change. As they watched, so they went quiet … and the crowd began to go quiet too. It was an incredible exercise in reverse psychology. Franny and Mike hogged all the limelight and I'm sure it made Gornik wonder a little bit about the return game.

They had given the impression that we were delighted to have got away with a two-goal defeat and I can only assume that the home side felt the two City men were showing they believed we could finish off the job at Maine Road.

When we played the second leg at Maine Road, we had five players out through injury. I turned out at centre-forward that night and we had quite a few young players in our side. Straight from the kick-off, the Poles swept down the right wing and when a Gornik man rattled the ball against a post – not a City player had got a touch to the ball in that opening attack – I thought: 'My God ... here we go again.' But we were much more at home on that muddy pitch than we had been on the skating rink in Katowice and our youngsters gave everything they had got. Ian Mellor scored a goal just before half-time and, ten minutes after half-time, I knocked home the goal which made the aggregate score 2-2. I scored again – at least I got the ball into the Gornik net – but the goal was disallowed. Still, we had done well enough to force a play-off, so we were satisfied.

The Poles weren't happy, though, especially when we won the play-off in Copenhagen 2-1 and it seemed that they had accused us of taking drugs before the second leg at Maine Road. At any rate, after the Copenhagen decider, two of our players, Colin Bell and David Connor, were called upon to take dope tests. There wasn't much of a problem for Dave, but unfortunately we couldn't say the same for Colin. On the day of a game, Colin Bell has nothing to drink and maybe only a small steak to eat. That lasts him from morning until night. He went into the room to take the dope test and we waited for him to come out. The match had ended shortly after 9 o'clock and it wasn't long before Dave came out. But at 11 o'clock, Colin Bell was still inside the little room. The problem was that Colin simply couldn't fill the bottle, or even make a token gesture.

The officials in charge of the dope test wouldn't let Colin drink even a Coke, in case it flushed traces of drugs away, so all he could do was his best ... and it was around 11pm when he finally turned up at the hotel. Colin was my room-mate and I'd been waiting for him so that we could spend a few hours on the town. He was so thoroughly disgusted with everything when he arrived that he declared his intention of going to bed, but after another half-hour he changed his mind ... and around 4.30am, when he had become well and truly rehydrated and that was the end of another excursion into Europe.

It was around this time I was called up for what would have been the greatest honour of my career – playing for England in the 1970 World Cup. The FA called me to say I was in the England squad to go to Mexico but around that time my wife Cheri had developed tuberculosis. Back then it was an illness that regularly killed people so needless to say I pulled out of the squad some three months before the tournament was due to start and stayed by her bedside until she made a full recovery. At the time being away from her and our baby daughter Natalie was unthinkable. Of course it was disappointing – I think Peter Storey took my place – but family always came before football for me.

6

CHAMPAGNE SUPERNOVA

MALCOLM ALLISON
(3RD JUNE 1969)

Four years ago it was all Man United, Man United, Man. United. It drove me mad. If I mentioned Man City they laughed at me. Who's laughing now?

MALCOLM ALLISON was a big fellow, in every way. Six feet tall, broad-shouldered and a man who could dominate the conversation no matter how many people were involved – especially if the topic was football. His image was made up of smoking big cigars, splashing out on champagne and generally doing things in a big way. A lot of people have said a lot of things about Big Mal over the years. He came from nowhere, really, to take charge of coaching at Manchester City and he went a long way, making many friends as well as some enemies. The enemies have laughed at his misfortunes through the years; the friends have defended him many times – and he has needed friends in football.

Malcolm's private life has made headlines more than once and some would say that all those years of living the high life have finally caught up with him as he struggles along today a shadow of his former self, but I'm not concerned with that side of his life. To me he was always a football character and our relationship in the game was what mattered. If you could get him talking football, he really opened up. He was a man's man and as a coach he was amongst the very best and that was a fact nobody could dispute. When City had won, he was on top of the world; when we had lost, he would go very quiet.

When he first arrived he completely changed the training routine. Previously we had just been doing laps but with the new methods and ideas Mal introduced, it meant that what had been a chore was now something all the players looked forward to and I'd even go as far as saying we couldn't wait to get to the ground and get started. Whilst he was original and inventive with his methods, he was also without doubt the best motivator I've ever known, which in itself is a form of coaching. He made you feel like a million dollars and you'd do anything for him. Typically, he'd kneel down in front of you with his hands on your knees and then tell you how good a player he believed you were. He'd say you were better than anyone else and that now was the time to go and show just how good you were. We'd step out on the pitch believing we could achieve anything as individuals and even more so as a team and the results spoke for themselves.

On the social side, Malcolm set the nightclubs to life in Manchester, especially the Piccadilly Club. The compere there was called Gerry Harris and he was a big West Ham supporter who knew Mal from his days in London. It was amazing to see the effect he was having on the people around him. I used to go in clubs every now and then and I can't ever recall seeing anyone drinking champagne but, two weeks after Malcolm's arrival, everyone was drinking the stuff. He was a handsome bloke, too and the women used to flock around him. I remember talking one day with his wife, Beth. She said that one evening Mal went out for some fish and chips wearing just a T-shirt and slippers. She didn't see him again for three days! I asked her what she said when he returned and she said that she asked him if the chips were still hot!

He could be a moody sod at times but, then again, he could be just the opposite – ebullient, ultra-confident to the point when, as they say, pride goes before a fall. Big Mal took a few tumbles in his time but, even into his seventies, his blood is still in the game he loves, even stating he could save his beloved Blues when a crisis loomed several years ago. Noel Cantwell, a former team-mate of Malcolm's at West Ham, once said of him: 'He must be one of the best coaches in the game. He's very enthusiastic … a man whose enthusiasm rubs off onto the players in his charge.' I'll go right along with that assessment. His restless energy was infectious, his knowledge of the game commanded admiration and his ideas were always fresh and interesting.

He kicked off his career with Charlton, spent several years as a player with West Ham and, at one time, suffered a lung problem which curtailed his playing career. He managed a Surrey team of non-Leaguers called Sutton United, was an official coach to Cambridge University, became manager of Bath City, moved on to Plymouth … and then he turned up at Maine Road. It soon became clear that his almost fierce involvement with football could make or break a team. In City's case, it made us, though his second spell at the club ultimately proved disastrous. I often wonder if his burning passion to make the Blues the best was a way of compensating for the fact that he had seen his own playing career come to a full stop, without it ever having scaled the heights.

I'm sure he wanted to prove that if he hadn't been an international star, he could turn other players into world-class material. Certainly more than one of the footballers at Maine Road owed part of their rise to international stature to the tuition and guidance of Malcolm Allison. If there was ability there, Big Mal would make sure that it really blossomed. I am sure that Mike Summerbee and Franny Lee, for instance, would be among the first to acknowledge the part Malcolm played in their graduation to England status. Mike played on either wing or at centre-forward and he could do just as good a job in one position as in the other. He was skilled when it came to beating opponents, brave when it came to meeting them head-on.

Franny loved to run at defences and he also became one of the biggest names in the game.

I felt that there was one thing which did upset Malcolm. No matter how hard he tried (and he did try), he could never get as close to Colin Bell as he did to Mike and Franny who he became very good friends with socially. At that time, Bell was probably the most talked-about player in the country for his world-class potential. Yet, instinctively, he was an average working class lad like Alan, Glyn and myself. I think it hurt Malcolm that he couldn't get closer to Colin and that he always seemed to be just an arm's length away from knowing what really made him tick.

I believe that if Malcolm had restricted his relationships with individual players in the team and made it more of an all-round thing, he might have been the manager of Manchester City for far longer than he actually was. His involvement with a section of the players, rather than with the whole squad, didn't show on the park but we talked about it amongst ourselves. Malcolm had a genuine belief in the ability of the team and I think he felt there was nothing we couldn't achieve with his coaching expertise at the back of us. He used to proclaim his faith in us to the point where it sometimes became an embarrassment – and we found that it could rebound on us. This happened when we qualified for Europe one season and Malcolm boasted that City would terrorise the opposition from the Continent. Maybe he genuinely believed this; maybe he thought that giving our ego a boost might put the foreigners in mortal fear, at the same time. But a Turkish team called Fenerbahce proved that even Mal wasn't quite ready for the European experience.

We met them first at Maine Road and were a side which, to be honest, we should have seen off comfortably. Instead, we missed so many easy chances of scoring that we could hardly believe it ourselves. When we played the return game in Turkey, we not only got kicked off the park ... we got kicked out of Europe.

Mike Summerbee and Franny Lee urged Malcolm more than once to lower the key and adopt a quieter profile and we all felt that he was making every match we played into a grudge match with our opponents. This meant we were having extra pressure put on us – and needless pressure at that. Mal's boasts were also having the effect of firing the other team's boilers and a graphic illustration of this came when we played Liverpool at Anfield. Mal proclaimed before the match that he was going to crack the Bill Shankly myth and subsequently Liverpool won the match comfortably and should have scored ten.

We once played a League Cup tie at Bury and didn't see Mal until shortly before the match began. We saw him only fleetingly once the game was over, as well. In between, I spent 90 minutes sitting on the bench watching Bury running us ragged and beating us 2-1. At that time, Joe Mercer had gone and Mal was the manager – the man at whom the buck stopped. Johnny Hart, who later took over for a time as the team boss, was taking us for training and there were times when the club and the players were thankful he was still around. Johnny knew more about City than anyone. He had been there many years and he never stabbed anyone in the back. Sometimes we didn't see Mal for days at a time and, when he did appear again, it would be training as usual, without a word of explanation as to where he had been.

Mal, of course, was the man who instigated the £200,000 transfer of Rodney Marsh from QPR to Manchester City. At the time, it was one of the most traumatic periods the club suffered – and City have known a few turbulent times during their history and, to be fair, much worse since.

7

OH, RODNEY RODNEY!

MIKE SUMMERBEE
(1990)

Rodney, at the time, wasn't the player for us.

MIKE DOYLE
(2003)

Rodney Marsh? Don't even get me started on him!

THE CITY FANS used to serenade Rodney Marsh with their version of Chicory Tip's massive hit 'Son of My Father' but for me, Rodney was singing the wrong tune when he stepped out to play for Manchester City. When he arrived in 1972, the season was drawing towards its close and we were bang on course for the First Division championship. Frankly, I think there was a large measure of divided opinion about signing Rodney from QPR in the first place – but Malcolm was adamant that he was just the player City needed. I came to the conclusion that Joe was against bringing Rodney to Maine Road.

Whatever the ins and outs of the situation, Malcolm got his way, as he invariably did. I suspect that he saw in Marsh the answer to George Best, who had a charisma all of his own and was a powerful pulling card for Manchester United. Possibly he felt that Rodney, a player of genuine flair who on his day could excite and entertain, would help to combat the Best appeal to fans and maybe he also believed that, as a team, City would be enriched by the sort of contribution Rodney Marsh could make.

At that stage of the season, we were about three points clear of the other leading contenders for the title and we were playing really well. Derby were the greatest threat, but they had one or two difficult matches to play, including a game against Liverpool. So long as we kept on turning in the sort of performances we had been doing, it was difficult to see anyone stopping us from claiming the title. And Malcolm, running true to form, made no secret of his belief that the championship trophy was coming to Maine Road. When Rodney arrived, it didn't take a genius to work out that he didn't really want to be pitched straight into action and needed time to adjust to what was a big move in more ways than one. On the other hand, Mal appeared to be determined to play him at the earliest possible moment. That, of course, meant someone had to make way.

We were playing Chelsea and that was the game in which Rodney made his debut. Tony Towers lost his place that day and, though Tommy Booth headed the only goal of the game, we recognised that we had achieved victory only by the skin of our teeth. It had been a lucky bonus for us and the pattern of our play began to disintegrate as the next few games went by. Marsh was a stone overweight and I told Malcolm exactly what I thought about his decision to leave Tony Towers out, who had been playing better than any of us. From the moment Marsh stepped on the pitch for City, the team began to go backwards. He had fantastic ability but was only worried about himself.

We had been a team which just poured forward and, in Franny Lee, Mike Summerbee and Colin Bell, we had three of the best attackers in the business. But, suddenly, they were getting into positions ... and the ball never arrived. Everyone seemed to end up by running into a blind alley. We seemed to be going backwards. Although Rodney was left out of the team after the Chelsea match, it soon became plain that Malcolm was determined to have him reinstated. You couldn't blame Marsh for the situation that was developing – he was the man caught in the crossfire, as it were. However, the problem for the rest of us was this: City were top of the League … and we had players worrying about who was going to be left out next time to make way for the new arrival, instead of being able to concentrate on consolidating and making sure no one else overtook us.

Everything at that stage should have been played low key, with no one concerned about anyone but the opposition and how to beat them, game by game. I must admit that while I wasn't the first player to be axed, I had felt rumblings of what was going to happen from the moment Rodney joined us, because Malcolm's attitude towards me appeared to have changed completely. I felt it was a bit of a strain for him even to say good morning to me and, deep down, I believed that he had already made up his mind that I would finally be the player who made way for his star signing. At the same time, I felt that Malcolm didn't really have the courage to come straight out and tell me that I wasn't figuring in his team plans. I felt he was trying to get his message across by unsettling me. Certainly I was convinced that something was the matter. Mal was always one for shouting a lot when we were having training sessions, but it seemed to me that there was a change of tone in his voice when he was telling me to do something.

We played Manchester United in a derby game at Old Trafford and Rodney was on the bench, but Mal had already indicated before the match that at some stage he would send on the substitute and, even before I went on the field, I had that lurking suspicion that I would be the man who would be taken off. In fact, at the start, I turned to Glyn Pardoe and said: 'I'll be lucky if I last the 90 minutes.' Before the game, Mal had talked about my having received a slight strain during a training session, so it seemed obvious to me which way the wind was blowing.

United scored first, but we equalised and we were starting to get really on top. I thought we would give them a good thrashing which was always especially sweet in their own back yard. But just after half time, the inevitable happened – I was brought off and Rodney went on. I felt so sick about it that I went straight to the bath. In fairness to Malcolm, I should add that City won 3-1 and I was glad for the team that we had scored a victory over United. But it didn't make me any happier about what had happened to me.

Was I prejudiced against Rodney? I don't think so. I've always believed that football is a team game and I was a team man throughout my career. My job was to play football to the best of my ability – not just for myself, but for the team as a whole with ultimately the club prospering. We'd had a lot going for us at Maine Road and we had built up a real spirit of comradeship, on and off the field. Everyone was geared to making it a team effort.

Marsh, I thought originally, was another extrovert, like Malcolm. He was so out of the ordinary it wasn't true. He appeared to me to try to be a law unto himself out there on the park, whereas if he had played first and foremost as a team man, there would have been no finer player anywhere. To me, it's a complete waste of time if a player has skill in abundance – and nothing else to offer. Rodney, I felt, was a Marsh man and not a City man. You simply couldn't do the tricks he did on a football pitch and maintain that you were a team man. He had marvellous skills, but so many times those skills were not used for the benefit of the side as a whole. It was infuriating to see him trying to 'nutmeg' opponents instead of laying off a simple pass. You got the impression – well, I did, at any rate – that he got more pleasure out of showing he could slip the ball between an opponent's legs than out of scoring a goal which could mean two points for the team. It was entertaining to watch for the fans but it began to affect us adversely.

Often enough, he would be turning on the box of tricks around the middle of the park, or even in his own half of the field. I maintained then, as I do now, that if Rodney had been dazzling the opposition in their own 18-yard box, he would have guaranteed himself 25 goals a season and remember that the only way to win titles is to make it a team success.

Throughout Manchester, there was controversy as to whether or not Marsh was the man for us. There was speculation as to whether he would stay in Manchester, or return to London ... and I must admit that it couldn't have been easy for him to feel settled, knowing he was the subject of such heated debate. Marsh stayed, but at the end of the season, it was Derby County who were crowned League champions and to my dying day, I shall remain convinced that City should have won the title, if only we had played it cool with regard to Rodney. If he had been given time to adjust to his new surroundings, given time to settle down and maybe ease his way into the side, things might have gone differently. But he was pitched straight in at the deep end and I don't believe that was the best thing for him or for the club. Then again, was he actually that good anyway?

I played with him in an England Under-23 side that also included Peter Osgood, Alan Stephenson, Glyn Pardoe and Colin Bell and, after about twenty minutes, I wondered what exactly it was he was trying to do. Ultimately, I reckoned that he wasn't fit to lace the boots of Peter Osgood, who I believed was a fantastic player. You never heard that much about Osgood but believe me, he was five times the player Marsh ever was – maybe if we'd signed him instead of Rodney, we would have probably gone on and won the league in 1973, not that Chelsea would have ever let him go.

No, whichever way you look at it, Marsh was a bad buy for City. I once played golf with Joe Mercer over at Hoylake where he was a member. He'd play a round or two with me and, as I was captain, he'd ask me questions about the side. My nickname was Tommy, after my dad, and he said to me: "Tommy, I didn't want to sign Rodney Marsh." I asked if

Malcolm had influenced his decision and he nodded. "You know, Tommy, I love Malcolm to pieces and he said to me he thought Marsh would take 6,000 off the gate at Old Trafford.

"Six thousand?" I said. "Boss, you get 7,000 watching the fucking grass grow at Old Trafford." He smiled and reiterated that he hadn't wanted to sign him and I think that had something to do with Marsh's lifestyle. The team that Joe had basically raised from kids were all team players who mostly were local lads who wanted to work for each other but Marsh just didn't fit into the ethos of that squad. Rodney and his showboating on the wing were affecting our whole game plan.

The one thing that really turned most of the lads against him – me in particular – was after the League Cup final against Wolves in 1974. We'd been beaten fair and square by Wolves 2-1 and had Tony Towers played for us instead of making way – again – for Marsh, I think it would have been a different result. After the final whistle we went to collect our tankards with Mike Summerbee the captain on the day. We stood in a line when Wolves went to lift the trophy and clapped them when they came down and we shook hands with each player. Mark Bailey, the Wolves captain asked me "What's up with him?" I looked around and Marsh was sloping off towards the dressing rooms. He hadn't collected his tankard or applauded the winners and that wasn't what we as a team were about.

At the evening reception, Marsh was out of order again. We all had collar and tie on but he came down with no tie and no socks on – maybe not the crime of the century but it was further testament to the theory that he was an individual doing his own thing – just like on the field of play. He looked ridiculous and he was the only player who didn't stand during the national anthem, which again, didn't go down well with the rest of the lads. Perhaps it had been alright at Fulham, but not at Manchester City. Whatever his personal thoughts on royalty or dress codes were irrelevant at times like that because he was meant to be representing the club but Rodney Marsh only ever really represented Rodney Marsh and everyone else could go and get stuffed as far as he was concerned.

The differences between him and me were numerous but the main one was that every time I went out to play for City I gave everything I had and wanted to win. I didn't want to fuck about; I just played the way I played which was hard but fair. I've never been one for show ponies – but I used to enjoy playing against them, believe you me.

He had an attitude I didn't like, to be honest and to explain that, I'll recall an incident that left a sour taste in my mouth. He was looking for somewhere to live and I offered to show him around. We set off in his Lotus and I remember showing him some of the houses in South Manchester where a lot of the lads lived. We were near Sale and he made a remark about the area being "nothing like down south" and that it was "more like a council estate." That didn't go down well with me at all and I took it as a dig at Manchester people. He was popular on the terraces – I'm not saying he wasn't – but the majority of fans who knew their football knew in their hearts that he wasn't good for the side.

Tony Book had taken over as boss when Rodney's career at Maine Road began to wane. One of the defining moments in his demise came against Burnley at home when, at half time, the assistant manager Ian McFarlane gave him the biggest bollocking I have ever seen any player get. He called him an 'absolute disgrace' and added that he felt he'd let himself down and his team-mates down, not to mention the people who'd paid to watch and from that moment on, there was no way back. Marsh had been awful, prancing around and just not interested and McFarlane had been spot on – not one player stood up for Rodney and that was because they all felt the same way. In the end, it was good riddance to him.

Shortly after, Tony Book made me captain and then said could I go and chat to the press about the appointment. I agreed and went down to the waiting journalists and told them I was delighted at being made skipper. Then some of them asked me about Marsh so I gave him a good slagging off, which, to be fair, I felt justified in doing. I said it was probably the best thing that could have happened to the club and the best thing for Rodney, for that matter. The next day the headlines read: 'Doyle Slates Lazy Marsh!' I suppose from that day to this, Rodney Marsh hasn't had much time for me but I haven't lost any sleep about it.

In the end Rodney returned to London. During his time at Maine Road, he gave many supporters a great deal of pleasure with his style of entertainment, but showmanship isn't what makes champions, as a general rule and the chairman of the club, Peter Swales, did say himself long after it was all over that Marsh should have been allowed to leave much sooner than he did. The way we threw the First Division title down the drain still leaves a bad taste in my mouth. Now Rodney sits on a panel for Sky Sports every Saturday, so good luck to him. He's made himself a good career and I don't begrudge him anything. As for Malcolm Allison, the man who signed him, there was one thing he did for which I can never forgive him, because it turned my life upside down for a spell. Worse still, it almost meant that I broke with Manchester City.

8

STAND UP IF YOU HATE MAN U

I WAS RIGHT – MIKE DOYLE
(DAILY EXPRESS, 28TH MARCH 1970)

*City's victory bore out the midweek boasting of right-half Mike Doyle
who claims that nowadays there is only one team in Manchester –
City. "Well I told you," he said after the match. "But that was even
easier than I expected." Explaining why he mockingly went in front of
the Stretford End with uplifted arms after one of City's goals he said:
"They had been jibing at me because of my views about United last
week – so I thought I'd go and give them some medicine back and
remind them that all I said was true."*

MIKE DOYLE
(THE SUN, 22ND MARCH 1999)

*We were gutted the year we got United relegated – while they were
on the fixture list, it was a guaranteed four points a season.*

IT'S EASY FOR me to trace back the origins of my hatred for
Manchester United FC because it happened when I was a kid.
The seeds were sewn at school where it seemed the
playground was a breeding ground for glory-hunting Reds.
They knew I was a City supporter and enjoyed taunting me
about how United were this, that, the other. It just made me a
stauncher Blue and even more determined to be part of
changing the face of football in this city. As time went on, I
signed for my idols and was part of a great team that
habitually thrashed United. Of course I taunted them
mercilessly and ended up having my windows put in, tyres
slashed and even received death threats, which I'll come to

later. I knew I must have been doing something right if I'd managed to get up the noses of so many people and I'd become the man all United fans loved to hate.

The earliest public haranguing I was aware of came when City's youth team won through to a cup semi-final showdown with United. We knew they were a very good side and we did okay but one of the goals involved me clearing a ball only to see it rebound of Alf Wood's knee and into the net for an own goal. Later, George Best, who was in the Reds' youth team later claimed I had 'cried like a baby' because I'd scored an own goal – which was of course incorrect, but why let the facts get in the way of a good story? Ever since that day, Manchester United were not top of my Christmas card list. To be fair, later on George, Mike Summerbee and me used to knock around together and at one time Buzzer owned a red and white Triumph and George owned a sky blue Alpine. As time went on and George's fame rocketed, he brought the story up and I thought well, if you can say things like that about me, it must be open season, my old mate. I felt quite within my rights to wind-up United on a regular basis because I was part of a team who could back my boasts up. Despite all the flack I was getting, I'd decided to follow the old adage 'in for a penny, in for a pound'.

So it may be all the more odd to hear that I once came so close to leaving Manchester City and signing for Manchester United, the team who were the antithesis of all I believed in. Even now, when I look back on the whole episode, it scarcely seems to be real. Even my wife said to me at the time 'You wouldn't have the cheek to do it … would you?' Not only did I have the cheek – I was ready to turn my back upon Maine Road and Malcolm Allison. I was hurt, disillusioned and somewhat bitter. As I said, the episode is one for which I can never forgive Mal

I've explained how my personal feud began with the Reds

but there was another episode that proved to me that it didn't matter how successful City were, the national media was obsessed with Manchester United and I was dog tired of it all. Thirty years on and it's worse than ever! Credit was due to City for being the last English club left in Europe but did we get it? Did we hell. City had been competing in the European Cup Winners Cup and we played the West German side, Schalke 04, in the semi-finals. They had some star international players in their ranks, so they were no mugs and it was a tie that could have easily gone either way. We lost that leg of the semi-final 1-0, but we played magnificently. That same night, Manchester United had a match too, a testimonial against one of the Bristol clubs if memory serves me right. When we boarded the plane for home at Düsseldorf airport next morning, we bought the papers and the back page headlines were about Manchester United – 'Reds Come Roaring Back' or something along those lines, while our game – a crucial European tie, remember – rated a small piece on an inside page. That pissed me off no end as it did the other lads. Mike Summerbee was the first to give the hacks, who seemed intent only on having a good piss-up, a piece of his mind and he went absolutely ape-shit. One of the chief culprits was Bob Russell from the Daily Mirror who had actually covered our game but we had about a paragraph's worth of coverage – unbelievable but I suppose entirely predictable.

I began having a go at Bob Russell, too. 'It's fucking ridiculous and I'm sick to death of this shite you lot peddle!" Russell began to tell me some lame excuse about deadlines and I said: "I couldn't give two fucks, basically." He asked me if that was the case, why didn't I tell him what I really thought about United. "I can't fucking stand them, simple as that." I told him bluntly. I thought, was the end of it. I'd blown my top and it was finished. But the next day in the newspapers my outburst was the now the back-page headlines – 'Doyle Hates United!'

It didn't go down at all well with a section of the populace in Manchester and much of London. During the course of the next week or two, I found that some folk had it in for me and they were ready to exact vengeance their way. I went to my parked car one day and found a dent in it and the car aerial snapped off. I had windows broken at my home and I received some, shall we say 'abusive' letters. I'd had enough by this time and I thought, well, bollocks to it. If this was the way they wanted to play it, I'd redouble my efforts to wind them all up even more. Gerald Sinstadt called me to go on ITV's Kick Off on the lead up to the derby game. I used to go on and say we were too good to lose to United and that we'd stuff them. I thought I might as well say it like it was, especially whilst these lunatics were making my life difficult – why not? I said Best was always in Book's pocket and the only decent player they had was Bobby Charlton. In fact what I was saying was absolutely true. I think I played 22 games against United and Best scored in only one of them – and that was after 14 seconds thanks to an error by yours truly but we still went on to win 3-1.

Then came the derby game against United. I'd been out with my wife for a meal and when we returned home, there were two men hanging around the house. I thought it meant more trouble in store, so I told my wife to stay in the car and lock the doors and I fished under the dashboard and picked up a heavy torch. Then I got out, prepared for trouble. As I moved to meet the men, I recognised one of them. He was the local CID chief. He said: 'Don't jump to conclusions and don't panic. Can we go inside?' I wondered what the hell was going on and when we had sat down in the house he explained the situation. A national newspaper had received a telephone call from a man saying that it was in the interests of my own safety if I didn't play in the derby game at Old Trafford the following Saturday. 'Otherwise, someone will take a shot at you.'

The CID chief was obviously taking the threat seriously.

'We'll have a man on the door of your home at night,' he said. The longer I tossed and turned in bed, the more worried I became. I kept getting up and going to the window and the sight of a police car outside didn't help me to think of it as a joke. In fact, I began to think that some lunatic really was out to get me. When I went down to the ground for training, two policemen accompanied me and they went back with me when I returned home. The same thing happened on the Friday and on the day of the game they remained unobtrusively in the background. Nothing happened though and once the game had got under way I began to forget my fears as I concentrated on the job in hand. At the end, I was still alive and kicking and that seemed to be that.

But on the Monday morning, I received a phone call from the police to say that they had picked up a man the previous night. It seemed that they had a description of someone who was wanted for a 'job' and a man answering the description had been spotted making a call from a public phone box. When the policeman went to question the man, he dropped the phone and ran. One of the Panda car coppers gave chase and caught him and the other picked up the dangling phone to see whom the man had been calling. The voice at the other end of the line told him it was a newspaper office – apparently the man had rung the office for a second time, to renew his threat to shoot me. But that really did mean the end of the affair, for I heard nothing further from the police or anyone else.

There came a point where I began to get a bit sick of this 'hatred' business, but I had to live with the reaction it had sparked off and I found myself wishing the whole thing had never happened – it was embarrassing more than anything to be honest. I remember being in a chippy on Oldham Road with Nobby Stiles and there was a bloke and his mate behind us and I could tell he was flabbergasted I was mixing socially with the enemy. Then I attended the opening night at Colin Bell's restaurant in Radcliffe, 'The Bell-Waldron'. Joe Mercer was there and so were one or two of the United players. Joe collared me and said: 'Have you got five minutes? I want you to meet someone' … then he led me round a corner and there were Sir Matt Busby and his wife. It was the first time in my life that I had met him to speak to and in view of all the publicity about my dislike of Manchester United, I felt somewhat tongue-tied. I didn't know what to say or where to look. I felt about six inches tall.

The United boss (he was still the manager then) stood up and shook my hand. 'I'm pleased to meet you,' he said, smiling. He could see I was nervous and embarrassed and he showed great understanding of my situation by adding "Don't worry – don't you change a thing.' Then he switched the conversation around to mutual friends and inquired about my family. He never mentioned the United business once. When I bumped into Joe Mercer later, he was chuckling away and I told him: 'You're a right bastard!' I met Sir Matt many more times after that and the more I saw of him, the more I came to admire him. He always found time to have a few words with me and I think he was a wonderful man.

We had beaten United that season in both the derby matches – 4-0 at Maine Road and 4-1 at Old Trafford – and I learned another lesson from Sir Matt after our victory on their ground. We were waiting in the team coach and our physiotherapist, Peter Blakey, had not arrived, so I nipped back up the stairs to tell him we were all set to go. On the way I passed Sir Matt, who shook my hand and said: 'Well played.' Then he added: 'You're putting it over us at the moment … but it all goes round in cycles. Our turn will come again.' And, of course, he was right – unfortunately – though it's just about time for City to take the ascendancy again, isn't it?

There was one incident that was anything but friendly in one derby match and I maintain that had I not been restrained I could have been set for a spell in Strangeways. What infuriated me so much was George Best's horrific tackle on Glyn Pardoe which broke his leg and effectively ended his career. Glyn was and still is a great mate and when I saw Bobby Charlton holding Glyn's leg up after the tackle I went after Best and had him around the throat. Had Tony Book and Brian Kidd not intervened I think I would have probably killed him. Was it a malicious tackle? Well, if you see the photograph of the tackle you can see Best is flying into the tackle towards Glyn's leg – there was no way he could win the ball coming in at that height. The next three tackles I made on Best were explosive – but fair – and he looked shaken and hurt which was utterly my intention. Tommy Docherty could see what was coming and took Best off. Maybe Best had thought it was me he was tackling because it defied belief – Glyn was a gentle man and hadn't an ounce of malice in his body.

Now to the Malcolm Allison episode, the one which came so close to changing the course of my career. When he left me out of the City side and put Rodney Marsh in, I went in to see Mal and he told me: 'Your attitude is all wrong.' I trained as hard as anyone and really enjoyed it, so I knew no one could accuse me of shirking in that respect. I also sweated blood for the Blues when I was wearing the jersey – it was generally acknowledged that I lived and breathed for the club. In fact, I wanted so much to be a part of the team that I voluntarily used to go back in the afternoons and put in extra training sessions on my own. So what was it all about, Malcolm?

I thought there was more to his attitude towards me than met the eye and I was convinced of this when he called me into the office and said: 'Stoke City want to buy you.' I countered: 'Do you want to sell me?'

'I don't want to sell any good players,' he replied

'Do you want me to go? Yes or no?' I demanded. He didn't answer me and, at that moment, my respect for him dwindled to the point of vanishing. I walked out of his office, went on the park and did my training, then marched back to see him. He told me that Stoke boss, Tony Waddington, wanted to speak with me on the phone. I asked what reason Malcolm had for wanting to sell me and he said: 'It's come to my notice that you've been causing a lot of unrest in the dressing-room.'

I looked Malcolm straight in the eye and said: 'You know as well as I do that that's bollocks.' Even though I would eventually, I decided there and then that I wasn't going to join Stoke City because I was convinced Malcolm was making a lame excuse to get rid of me. I felt that probably the deeper reason was that City wanted to get some money back to help balance the £200,000 they had splashed on Marsh. Maybe Malcolm was under pressure to recoup some of that cash – I don't know, because I never attended a boardroom meeting.

Out of courtesy, I spoke to the Stoke manager and I found him to be a real gentleman. But what set me even more against moving was the fact that he said Malcolm Allison had confirmed to him that I was up for sale. Only 30 minutes earlier, Malcolm had been telling me he didn't want to sell good players. I told the Stoke boss: 'To be perfectly honest with you, I'm going to say no to Stoke, straight away,' and that was the end of a projected £80,000 transfer from Maine Road … or so I thought.

When Malcolm asked me what I had decided, I told him straight: 'If I leave City, I'll chuck the game.' I had a garage business and I wasn't dependent on football for a living, nor did I want to play for any other club but the one I had known my entire career. I didn't owe them anything because I hadn't cost them a penny and it wasn't that I felt they owed me anything either. I just didn't want to play for another club if there was anyway I could remain with the Blues, even in the First Division – yet I was hurt when I thought that I was being allowed to leave without any explanation.

Malcolm told me not to be silly. But I had the bit between

my teeth and I was ready to turn my back on the game and the club I loved. I was selling my house at the time and the man at the estate agency who was handling matters was called O'Farrell.

The next thing that happened was my father-in-law told me a woman had been on the phone asking to speak to me. I hadn't been in, so he'd told her to ring back later. When the phone at the garage rang again, my father-in-law answered it and said: 'That woman's after you again.' I think he thought I was having an affair on the side. When I took the phone, a woman's voice said: 'Just a moment, I have Mr O'Farrell for you.' And when I heard a mans voice, I thought it was the estate agent and I said: 'Have you got rid of this bloody house yet?'

The voice replied: 'I think you've got the wrong O'Farrell. I'm the manager of Manchester United. I've heard that you are available.' I said: 'Well, it seems that way,' to which he replied: 'Well, I would very much appreciate it if you would come and play for me at Manchester United.'

When it sank in what he had said, I could hardly believe it. I had turned down Stoke a week earlier and now Frank O'Farrell, who had recently become the manager at Old Trafford, wanted me to 'cross the road' and play for City's greatest rivals. I reckoned it had to be a wind-up considering my views on all things red but it wasn't, which put me in a hell of a dilemma. I listened to the terms he was ready to offer me, and then I asked him if I could sleep on matters, before making a decision. I went home and told my wife what had happened and that I was actually considering joining United. She thought I was joking but soon realised it was for real. She said she would respect my decision but thought it would be a hell of a wrench to leave my boyhood team for the arch-enemy.

I tossed and turned all night and eventually came to the conclusion that if Malcolm was that keen to see the back of me, maybe it was time to move on, even if it was across the road. I had a family to feed and a career to get on with so the next day, I told Frank O'Farrell that he'd got himself a new player. I asked if he wanted me to come over the next day to sign.

'It can't be done that quickly,' he told me. 'I'll speak to Malcolm.' Then Frank O'Farrell rang me at the garage on the Sunday and told me: 'It's all arranged. I'll see you tomorrow.' So I had played my final game for Manchester City and I was going to exchange the blue shirt for a red one. I wondered what the media and the fans would make of it when the news broke. It would cause a sensation in Manchester football circles after all the hullabaloo I'd caused over the years between the clubs.

And yet I still couldn't believe it was about to happen. As I lay in bed that night, I suddenly realised that there hadn't been one telephone call from a journalist. Therefore my impending move to United must have been one of the best-kept secrets in football. Usually, no matter how hard a club tries to keep a transfer deal hush-hush, someone sniffs out the story and it breaks. But no one, it seemed, had got even an inkling of the deal between the two Manchester clubs. It was midnight and the phone hadn't rung all night. Yes, this is one top-secret deal that hasn't leaked out, I thought – or, more likely, maybe something else had happened. I reached Maine Road next morning at 10: 45, all set to be told to go across to Old Trafford. The rest of the players had gone training, but Malcolm Allison was in the dressing room, wearing training gear. He said: 'Good morning' and that was for the first time in about six months he had bothered to utter anything other than some snarled remark. Then he added:

'Come on, get your kit. We're going to Wythenshawe Park.' I didn't question him, but got changed, thinking that I must be scheduled to go across to Old Trafford later. On the way to the park, Malcolm didn't say one word about football – instead he began to talk to me about my garage business. I sat and listened and decided not to lower myself by telling him I was expecting to go to Manchester United that morning. If the deal was going to be off – and I had started to suspect this was the position – then Malcolm would have to do the explaining. I wasn't going to make it easy for him.

I did some training, returned to Maine Road, got bathed and changed and then Malcolm said: 'In for training as usual, in the morning.' He never mentioned Manchester United, never told me the transfer was off and that was the last thing I ever heard about it. My suspicions had been confirmed; I was staying at City. Frank O'Farrell never came back to me and it was as though the whole bizarre situation had never arisen. I simply went home ... and my wife was the first to refer to the matter, when she asked me: 'Well, have you signed?' All I could say was 'No.' When she asked me why not, I told her that nobody had uttered a word to me about it. I decided then and there that there was no way that Malcolm Allison was ever going to shift me out of the first team at City again.

I was going to play even harder than I had ever done before and prove Malcolm wrong about having been ready to sell me. My pride had been terribly hurt and I was determined I wasn't going to become a political pawn, as had happened in the past week or so. Later, I heard that several of the City directors had more or less intimated that if I did go to United it would only be over their dead bodies. That suited me just fine, I could just never see myself kissing the United badge.

9

THAT'S ENTERTAINMENT

MIKE DOYLE
(1984)
It was just a job but a bloody enjoyable one.

BERNARD MANNING
(2004)
For my money he was one of the greatest City players ever. Mike the Magnificent we used to call him – a man amongst men, great company ... wonderful company!

THERE WILL BE a number of City fans that recall Eddie Large being a regular fixture at Maine Road during the late 1970s. I became good friends with both him and Syd Little around that time and I used to play golf with Eddie down at Holdsworth. He was a huge City fan and a smashing bloke to get along. They were playing clubs at the time and packing out audiences everywhere, so I was chuffed when they got their big break on television and, for a time, they were the hottest act on the box with millions tuning into their Saturday evening show.

They were just two Manchester lads who had made good and the money and fame never changed them. Eddie moved down to Bristol after a while, but he still came up to see the Blues play every week and occasionally sat on the subs bench, which none of the players minded about. It was great to see someone off the box on the bench as it sometimes took a bit of tension out of situations. He even pooped into the dressing room from time to time but he was respectful and never said anything out of order. Syd was a City fan, too, but he could take it or leave it and wasn't bothered about attending every game like Eddie did.

Bernard Manning was another comedian I always got along well with. I went to the Embassy Club one evening and he got me up on the stage to sing – I've not got a bloody clue what it was – but whilst I was there I noticed he was sweating like a pig. I told him to get down to Platt Lane for some fitness training and thought no more about it. The following Monday he called me up and said: "Right, when are we doing this training, then?"

I had to laugh. I called up the local press and they sent down a photographer to see Bernard being put through his paces. I got him in the gym and had him circuit training and lifting weights and he had a few choice quips, as I'm sure you can imagine. I know he's controversial and his language is a bit choice on occasions – not that he gives two shits about that – but he remains one of the funniest men I've ever met.

I met a number of local celebrities during my time with the Blues and was heavily involved with charity work, particularly for the RNIB. I became quite pally with Ken Farrington who played Billy Walker in Coronation Street and we used to go out at least once a month. After a while, I invited a few of the United lads to come out with us and after a while we had a small group of celebrities helping out good causes and suchlike. I went to see Ken once in a play whilst I was in London with England and had a night out with him. I didn't really enjoy the play – it wasn't my cup of tea at all – no knickers or dancing!

Another Coronation Street star I got to know well was Anne Kirkbride who still plays Deirdre Barlow to this day. I did a lot of penny pushes with her and Eileen Derbyshire who plays Emily Bishop and got to know them socially in the process. Anne used to live near to me in Saddleworth at the time. In fact, she lived a few doors down from my favourite pub, The Old Original' that was owned by former Lancashire cricket player

Peter Marner who was another top bloke. I had many a good night in there, I can assure you.

I got to know a band member of Manchester band The Hollies, chiefly because he opened a club in Ashton around the corner from my house. But it was another local group who finally allowed the British public the dubious honour of having my dulcet tones on vinyl. Graham Goulden, Kevin Godley and Lol Creme from 10cc were all City supporters and they wrote a record called 'The Boys in Blue' for the club in 1972. We were invited down to Strawberry Studios in Portwood, Stockport to make a song that unbeknown to the lads at the time, would be sung before and after every home game to this very day.

It didn't look like a recording studio from the outside but inside it had everything you'd imagine it should have; mixing desks, glass booths, sythensizers and various instruments dotted around. The producer directed us and we all enjoyed the experience and were impressed when it was finally finished. I can still make out my own voice on the record and each time I hear it played it reminds of that era. I know it was released by RCA in 1972 but I don't think it made the charts. Most clubs release a song on the eve of a FA Cup final – not us – there was nothing in particular doing that season and therein probably lies the reason it didn't get us on Top of the Pops. Still, as football records go, it has stood the test of time and I'm proud to have been a part of it, even if you can still hear me go off-key at one point.

Mixing with celebrities wasn't always advantageous. I was asked to a charity event at Carriages which was a nightclub and trotting track. I was told showjumper Harvey Smith, who was a controversial but popular figure back then, would be there and I thought it would be good to meet him as he was painted as being quite a fiery character. What a boring fart he turned out to be – he had the personality of a wooden door and didn't have a clue how to make even the most basic conversation. Brian Kidd was with me and we were asked to have a trundle around the track with a pony and trap. Kiddo wasn't too struck on the idea and his ill-ease almost caused a catastrophe.

All we could see was the horse's arse in front of us and Kiddo reckoned it was going too fast and so pulled the reigns back. The horse quickly went from a canter into a sprint and we took off at speed. Kiddo tried to slow the horse again by the same method but it only made it go faster. A bloke jumped into another trap and pulled alongside us. "Drop the reigns!" he yelled at Kiddo. But he wouldn't because he had nothing to hold on to. We eventually came to a stop and Kiddo stepped out of the trap like John Wayne, muttering "that's the first and last time you'll get me on one of those fucking things."

I liked Kiddo and it was me that tapped him up at Arsenal. The boss Tony Book knew I was mates with Brian and asked me to find out if he was interested in joining City. He had heard on the grapevine he wasn't happy in London and it was my job to find out if it was true and sound him out.

I gave him a call.

"How are you doing?" I asked.

"I'm okay."

"How's your wife?"

"She's back in Manchester. I've got a bed, a television and a cooker and that's it."

"Oh, I see. Listen, Kiddo, I know you've always wanted to play for City, haven't you?"

"Eh?"

"You know, when you played for Manchester Boys, you always talked about playing for the Blues, didn't you?" I hoped I wouldn't have to spell it out to him and thankfully, I didn't.

"Right, got you," he said at last.

"When are you back in Manchester, then?"

"I'm coming up tomorrow."

"Okay, I'll meet you at the Grand Hotel."

I called Tony and told him what had been said and the next evening we all had a meal and a chat and Kiddo said he was up for it and signed shortly after. Sometimes, it's not necessarily what you know, but who you know. I liked Brian and he was great buy for the club. He should have played many times for England. He created space for himself and was difficult to mark and was hard with it, but fair. I've always got on well with him, even if he is a tight bastard. Kenny Clements was another tight get – he'd put 50p's worth of petrol in his car and I'd ask him what was the point? He'd just tell me that if someone stole his car, they wouldn't get very far! If only the City fans knew what their heroes were really like!

I enjoyed the life of a footballer but I realised it couldn't last forever and with that in mind, I entered the car business at the peak of City's success. It made perfect sense because I had the money to invest and, for a while, it was a great success.

It began with my father-in-law's interest in wheeler dealing cars, which he did almost as a hobby. He was a grocer by trade but when a friend who was in the motor business told us Hartshead Motors was up for sale, we decided to make further enquiries. I knew the brothers who owned the garage because I'd bought a couple of cars from them and we looked at what was on offer. There was room for about 20 cars in the showroom and the workshop was underground. There were also eight terraced houses included in the price so, after discussions with my father-in-law, we decided to buy the business. We had to pay £25,000 and also take on a £60,000 overdraft but we reckoned we could soon run Hartshead at a profit. I had saved about £26,000 so we talked to the bank, arranged all the legalities and went ahead with the deal. In just under 18 months, we had cleared the overdraft, built an extension, demolished the houses and extended the forecourt.

We now had room for 100 cars and there were also three

flats above the garage we rented out and 24 lock-up garages at the back which were also rented out. It was a great little business. We were a Triumph dealer and it was a great time for Triumph sales and we couldn't get them in quick enough. Our main supplier was Henley's but gradually they offered us less and less help with profit margins and we decided to change to Opal, which proved to be a sound decision. We were also one of the very first garages to supply Ladas and one model was a left-handed jeep. We had a farmer come in for a test drive and he paid in cash when we returned from putting the jeep through its paces. "Right lad," he said to me, "I'll have it. How much is it?' I told him it was £600 and he paid in cash there and then. Over the next few weeks we sold 28 of the same model – every time to a farmer! Word must have got around as they, pardon the pun, flocked in.

Ron Saunders bought an XJ6 off of me with about 3000 miles on the clock. It was immaculate and we had the car dropped off at his house only for him to call me about two hours later.

"Come and take this fucking car back," he demanded. "The knob's fallen off the radio." I must admit, the word knob was in my mind when I heard his voice. This was the manager of Manchester City and he couldn't even fix a radio knob. It just about summed him up, for me.

Eventually things began to get tight in the car game and we decided to sell up. We'd run it from 1970 to 1978 but I never took a wage from it. I was playing football and earning a good living so the garage provided an interest more than anything outside of football.

10

PEERS AND SOUVENIRS

MIKE DOYLE

Of course I'll be involved with Denis Law. Tell me someone who isn't during a derby game. And that goes for me, too. The more the Old Trafford crowd yell at me the more I like it.

PEOPLE OFTEN ASK me who were the players I admired most in my playing days and I would have to say Johnny Crossan was one of the best. He was perhaps one of the most talented players in the country when he was at City and he was a top bloke off the pitch, too. His razor sharp tongue had most of us in stitches in the dressing room and you'd best not take him on in a wind-up or you would end up the wounded party – he always had an answer and I mean always. One game at Burnley saw Alex Holder tackle Johnny who went tumbling over. Alex said, "All you are is a fucking jumper," to which Johnny relied; "Your wife is a better one, mate!" That shut him up and it was just one of dozens of similar quips he used to come out with.

Johnny always had a ready word for anyone and he could take care of himself, too. When we played Liverpool at Anfield once, Tommy Smith was giving Colin Bell a hard time and Johnny told 'Smithy' to 'behave himself'. Tommy was stung into answering: 'Come anywhere near me and I'll fill your face in.' To which the quick-witted Irishman replied: 'See me after the game and I'll give you a bucket of Polyfilla to fill yours in!' Johnny – one of the most skilful players I've seen, for close control of the ball – had a real ding-dong with Smith that day.

I was doing quite a bit of attacking that season and when I moved up field Glyn Pardoe did his usual covering job for me. It got so that the opposition could never be quite sure what was happening, because I was going through their defence from such deep positions. In fact, I scored nine goals in around half a dozen matches, winning City some vital points in the process.

At that time, I didn't believe City were receiving enough credit for what they were achieving, not just in terms of picking up points and winning trophies, but of how they were setting a new pattern for English soccer. England had won the World Cup in 1966 without wingers ... we were bringing wingers back into fashion, with Mike Summerbee on one flank and Tony Coleman on the other and we didn't have a rigid back-four line, either.

Tony Book, George Heslop, Glyn Pardoe, Alan Oakes and myself alternated as defenders. When I was up, Glyn was at the back, covering for me; when he went surging up field, I dropped back. Teams found it difficult to know what to do against us because they could never be certain how many City men would be pushing up and where the danger was likely to come from. Virtually everyone in the side was capable of scoring goals – Alan Oakes and myself, for instance, shared about 20 goals one season.

One of the lads I had an enormous amount of respect for during my career was Tony Book who was a first class player. When people ask me who were the best players I played against, I'd always say Bobby Charlton and Johan Cruyff. 'What about George Best?' they'd ask and I would tell them that in all the games I played against him, he never ever caused us any problems and the reason for that was Tony Book. Best thrived on defenders making the first move but Tony never did that and subsequently had the Irishman in his back pocket throughout the game. As I said earlier, he only scored one against us and we still ended up winning 3-1 and that was because of my mistake, not Tony's.

I think that if he'd been left alone when he was boss of City, he would have ended up being one of the best in the country because he was getting together a team that was looking like it was going to challenge for honours for many years to come. If we'd had a chairman other than Peter Swales, I believe he would have achieved great success, but he didn't. I don't think Peter Swales did any favours for Manchester City in his time as chairman. He was an egotist and a seventies version of Chelsea's Ken Bates and it was a sad day when Tony was sacked from his job. Tony still does scouting for Tottenham but I'm sure he would have led the club into a new era of glory had he been allowed to do so.

Denis Law was a wonderful striker and a tricky bugger, too. He was a slippery sod to play against and as easy going and laid back as he may have appeared, you'd have to be good to get one over on Denis – just ask Tony Towers. The Law-man had settled well after joining City for the second time in his career on a free transfer from over the road. He got on really well with Towers who was only about 19 or 20 at the time and they used to take the piss out of each other all the time. One thing Denis couldn't stand was cold water and he was always in the bath last. One of the communal baths was always really cold because the water drained off the roof of the Main Stand and was stored in tanks on top of the roof. Denis got into this bath and it was bloody freezing so he got straight out again complaining and Tony followed him out and aimed a hosepipe at him. Denis went mad and ran out, drenched with ice cold water. Shortly after he came back in dressed and ready to go and picked up the hose and gave Tony a cold shower, just like he'd had. Towers chased him into the toilet where Denis locked himself in. Towers put the pipe over the top of the door whilst Denis screamed inside. Towers got back into the bath and Denis left the room soaking. TT was having a laugh at his mate's misfortune –

until he came to get dressed. Denis had left his soaking clothes on Tony's peg and gone home in his dry clothes. Like I said, Denis was a wily old bugger.

Another great player and teammate was Neil Young. He was a wonderful talent but I can't recall him ever scoring with a header. Strange, that, because he was partner in head tennis and was one of the best around. We had a good night out once when we went over to play an exhibition head tennis match against Leeds in Yorkshire. The venue was packed with about 1,000 fans and they must have all expected an easy win for their heroes, Peter Lorimer and Johnny Giles, but we beat them 3-0 in a best of five series. We had battered them and I don't think the crowd could believe Neil Young's heading ability. After, we went out with the Leeds lads to the Nouveau Club and Billy Bremner and Norman Hunter came along for a drink, too. The Leeds lads really looked after us and we had a fantastic night. We were staying in a hotel for the evening so neither Neil nor I had to worry about getting home in a fit state. Later, Leeds boss Don Revie also stopped by and he seemed like a nice bloke, too.

During the years when the silverware kept coming to Maine Road, other teams used to try all they knew to take us down a peg. We were by far the better of the Manchester teams and it was embarrassingly one-sided in most derby matches played at that time. After we had won the championship and half a dozen trophies, other teams wanted to beat us so much more – and that was where Malcolm Allison helped to make a rod for our backs, with his claims about what we were going to do to the opposition. In the dressing room, the lads would sometimes say: 'I wish he'd keep his mouth shut.' Malcolm tried this tactic with Manchester United, when we were the top dogs in the city and his words often added fuel to the fire – even more than my solitary outburst had done. We never picked up a newspaper without expecting to see some big words from the big man. Strangely, he didn't say much to us about United, he left his 'major speeches' to functions and newspaper interviews. I remember one occasion when he made it clear that he considered he had done more in three years or so than Matt Busby had done in two decades ... and the Reds' boss was there when he said it. Balls were never something Big Mal was short of!

When Joe and Malcolm took charge at Maine Road, it was the signal for a signing spree. Mike Summerbee, Franny Lee, Tony Book, George Heslop, Colin Bell, Tony Coleman, Ken Mulhearn ... they all joined City to become first-team players.

Our gates doubled and for the first time in donkey's years the club was really going places. City's name kept cropping up in conversations between football fans and during the season we collected the championship of the Second Division, with only Southampton in real contention as rivals for the top spot.

We had won the title with three games to go, in fact and one of our final home matches of the season was against the Saints. We had both clinched promotion places and that match ended in a 0-0 draw, so honour was satisfied all the way round. Not many of the teams in Division Two were much good that season and we were by far the best side. The only doubt we had was as to whether we could hold our own during our first season back in the top flight. That was when we employed Tony Book to do a sweeper's job and he did it in his usual immaculate manner.

If we went into the First Division with some feelings of apprehension, we achieved what we had set out to do. We made sure there were no slips and that we didn't slide straight back to where we had come from. As I became acclimatised to the First Division scene it began to get through to me just how important it was that City should stay up. No matter what you have won at the end of one season, it's all forgotten once you get going again in the following season and so far as the fans and the football world at large are concerned, it's what the manager and his players achieve the next time out that counts. There isn't much room in football for living on past glories – you've got to get up and go again and be ready to scale new peaks. We had to show above all that we could compete in every sense with Manchester United.

United had their own superstar during City's glory years in Best and enough words have been written about this character to fill a library. I say his record speaks for itself but I still don't think he was a patch on Bobby Charlton. For me, Bobby was much more difficult to play against and we always seemed to have the answer to Best. Whenever there was a Manchester derby, Tony Book took care of Best for the afternoon.

Perhaps he was so ineffective against us because we were not afraid of him, as so many teams were. We didn't have any sort of a complex about him. The more we looked at films and analysed his play, the more we saw that defenders always used to commit themselves against him and go in with sliding tackles. That was when he left them floundering. It seemed to us that no one ever stood there and put the ball in his court – no one ever challenged him to make up his own mind as to which way he was going. But Tony Book used to do just that – and time and again he proved that when it came to the moment of decision he was quicker than George. Tony would stand there and Best would end up jumping over the ball half a dozen different ways before he really did anything positive and when George had committed himself, Tony was there in a flash.

Malcolm Allison must get the credit for being the first – in my book, anyway – to fathom out the way to stop George Best and Tony Book was just the man to carry out Mal's instructions to the letter. He was so cool, so quick, that he seemed to have a sort of jinx on the United star and I would guess that Book was the defender Best disliked most to play against, in fact, I think he has said as much in one of his autobiographies.

George seemed to me to be a Jekyll-and-Hyde character. You could meet him before or after a game and as you listened to his softly-spoken words, in that quiet Irish accent, it appeared that butter wouldn't melt in his mouth. He was pleasant to chat to, modest and extremely likeable. It was difficult to imagine that maybe only a few hours later his name would be making headlines for an off-the-field escapade. Frankly, it upset me that he should go the way he did, with all the ability that he so obviously possessed. All he needed to do was look after himself for another couple of years at United and I reckon he would have become the first football millionaire in the country and I know he earned a lot of money as it was.

I always felt it was a tragedy that a player with George Best's natural footballing gifts should have to say he was turning his back on the big-time arena because the pressures were too great. To my mind he built up many of the pressures for himself. I would have been more than happy to think I had been blessed with an eighth of the ability that George possessed. You couldn't help liking the guy, yet the way his career at Old Trafford finally foundered was something that should never have happened.

It's no secret that he caused the club and Sir Matt Busby acute embarrassment at time yet I don't think anyone would have dreamed that, in the end, any club would feel it had to give a free transfer to a player of such skill. He came back into the game with Fulham and did a job for them, but I still believe that Old Trafford should have been his stage until the day came for him to quit playing for good.

11

ROUND PEG, SQUARE HOLE

MIKE DOYLE
(MARCH 1974)

Let's face it, I'm a City fanatic. I'm the guy on the terraces who has been given the chance to put down his rattle and step out for the team he loves. I know my strengths and my limitations. I never hide. I never shirk responsibility. People have said to me that I should play for England. I never lose sleep about that. I'm just happy to play for Manchester City.

I'VE SEEN MANAGERS come and go at City and occasionally it has seemed as if the club was a stopping-off place for travellers passing through. Joe Mercer and Malcolm Allison had a good thing going for them when we were winning trophies. Later, the atmosphere obviously soured, although the players, wrapped up in their own side of things, didn't realise just how close the partnership was to breaking point. Joe's departure was like the wielding of a knife; when it came it was sudden and sharp and the break was clean. One day, we knew he was going; the next, he came in to see us and said his goodbyes. Then he was off.

Basically, we were glad about one thing: that the management of the club had remained 'in the family'. Outwardly, nothing changed – Allison didn't even refer to the fact that he was now the manager, although we all wished him the best of luck in his new job. There was a twinkle in Mal's eye and a tingle of expectancy about the place. I think everyone felt we were on the verge of even greater achievements. Then, before we knew what was happening again, Malcolm, too, was on his way to seek other pastures.

By that time, Tony Book was ready to call it a day as a player and he was named assistant manager, while Johnny Hart, that long-time servant of the club, stepped into the hot seat. I was pleased for Johnny, because he was one of the men I most respected at the club. In my heart of hearts, I wondered if he would be strong enough for the role he had just been given. I hoped he would be able to cope with all the strains that being manager of Manchester City brought with it, but I knew that his health hadn't been particularly strong, even before he was handed the role.

At the time Johnny assumed command, we were not having such a successful season – indeed, we were struggling a bit to avoid getting trapped among the relegation-threatened sides. His first game in charge came when we played Leeds at Maine Road. Johnny called me on to one side and asked me: 'How do you feel about playing sweeper?' I didn't fancy that much, but he told me: 'I want you to pick Allan Clarke up.' I agreed to do my best. Tony Towers scored the winner for us that day and I gave one of the best displays I have ever given. At that stage, we needed nine or ten points and we needed them badly; but by the end of the season we were comfortably safe … although our last home match saw us go down to a 3-2 defeat to Crystal Palace – by then being managed by a certain Malcolm Allison.

The pressures of being manager had become too great for Johnny and his health suffered even further. He finished up a victim of nervous exhaustion. When he had finally stepped down from the job, I asked him one day: 'Did you think you were right for it?' And Johnny, who had never shirked anything in all the days I had known him, answered: 'I wouldn't have been a man if I'd turned down the job. I had to find out for myself.'

The typical honesty with which he answered my question only increased my admiration for him and I was sorry he hadn't been able to survive the pitfalls and pressures. At the same time, all the players knew that while Johnny had been in charge, Tony Book had helped to take some of the strain and I think we were unanimous in the view that Tony could and should be the man for the top job. But the word filtered through on the grapevine that another fellow would be arriving to claim the vacancy. His name was Ron Saunders. He had done well whilst boss of Norwich, but he was regarded by some players as a strict disciplinarian. One of the men who played for him at Carrow Road once said: 'There are times when you hate his guts ... but when he tells you to go, you find you'll run through a brick wall for him.' Asa Hartford and Willie Donachie met a former City player, Ian Mellor, who had gone to Norwich and Ian had confirmed to them that Ron Saunders was a very tough cookie indeed. Some people described him as being like a sergeant major, although I have heard him express some surprise that folk should look upon him like that.

All I knew about Ron Saunders was what I had heard and the only judgement I could make about him was from having played against Norwich. Some people claim that a team is like its manager, in the sense that it plays the way the manager thinks. It has been said that in Ron Saunders' days as the team boss at Norwich, he had to make the best use of the players' strengths and I see nothing wrong in that, especially if there is no bottomless purse when it comes to recruiting new signings. My experience of playing against Norwich was limited, but I found them well-drilled and unimaginative. They seemed to lack real flair and the accent was more on the defensive than on the offensive.

The City players held a meeting and four of us – Willie Donachie Joe Corrigan Colin Barrett – and myself – were deputed to ask, through Tony Book, for a meeting with the chairman, Peter Swales. Tony Book said he would put our request forward – we hadn't told him why we wanted the meeting and quite frankly, I half-expected that we would receive word that the chairman couldn't see us, because of his other commitments.

However, back came a message that we should report for a meeting at the ground with the chairman the following morning at 10.30am. Again, I wouldn't have been surprised if we had got there and been told the chairman couldn't make it. But I completely misjudged the man. Not only was he there, but he was on time – and he invited us into the private boardroom at Maine Road. In all my time at the club, I had never even seen inside this room and I thought: 'Well, there's one thing about it … I've finally made it to the boardroom.' We were asked to sit down and the chairman sent for tea and biscuits. And then the talking began.

We didn't make any bones about our feelings – we said we had heard that he could be appointing Ron Saunders to manage the club. We had nothing against him in particular but we felt that the man we would like to see installed in the job was Tony Book. We believed that he had given evidence that he was capable of doing the job and we wanted him to have the chance. He was someone who had the confidence of the players. Peter Swales sat and listened, then he told us he would think about what we had said but as we thanked him for hearing us out and made our way from the boardroom, I think we all knew, deep down, that he had already decided upon Saunders as the next City manager – and that was exactly how it happened.

Tony Book remained the second-in-command, but I have to say that the chairman did things the right way. He called a meeting of the players and told us about Ron Saunders coming before any official announcement was made. He said he had considered the points we had made but that, in the end, he had come to the decision. He finished up by saying 'If I've made a mistake, it's on my own shoulders and I'll take the responsibility for it.' That was honest enough and when it had all gone wrong, Peter Swales had the guts to tell Saunders that it was time for the parting of the ways. All the players respected the chairman for his attitude on both occasions and I can only add that it took a lot of courage for the top man at the club to stick to his guns for a start and to hold up his hands at the end. My admiration for Swales would wane as time moved on and I don't think I was the only one who felt this way.

So Ron Saunders arrived, amid a blaze of publicity and we all waited to see how the land lay. We soon were of the opinion that he had taken the wrong attitude from the start and this, in fairness both to the players and to Saunders, made things twice as difficult as they should have been. We had expected some plain speaking, but I still think that the way he spoke to players such as Mike Summerbee, Denis Law and Franny Lee was out of order. It became plain that he was determined to do things his way and that, in the process, there were going to be some changes among the playing personnel.

He would come in and be very sarcastic. He began calling Denis Law 'the old man' and he referred to Franny Lee as 'Fatty'. Denis may have been past his best, but he deserved more respect than he was being given. As for Franny Lee, yes, he was chunkily built, with a barrel-like chest ... but he hadn't an ounce of spare flesh on him. He was solid muscle. In the case of Mike Summerbee, Saunders started off by making him skipper and ended up by almost selling him to Leeds United. Although Mike was named captain, the manager never seemed to have two words to say to him. It seemed to be simply a case of him saying to one of the most able and experienced players at the club: 'Well, you're the skipper ... you look after the players.' Mike told me later that he had spoken to Leeds and that Don Revie wanted him. Buzzer was only too ready to sign and escape the Saunders regime but, somewhere along the way, the price apparently went up and the deal was called off. Mike told me he felt so sick about this development that he was almost ready to quit the game.

Maybe we had a built-in prejudice even before Ron Saunders arrived at Maine Road but, even if we had, events after the new manager settled in did nothing to make us change our minds or alter the impressions we had already formed. Our first away game under his command involved an overnight stay and the club was always very good when it came to the fare we could have in the dining room. We could order what we wanted, within reason. One of the favourites, as far as I was concerned, was prawn cocktail followed by fillet steak but that night, as we all went into the restaurant, Ron Saunders told us: 'No prawn cocktails,' and we ended up eating off the set menu, which had never happened as long as I had been at the club. So the atmosphere was far from being one of genial friendship all round. Most players like to do their own thing on the night before a game and we all felt that we were grown-up people. Yet here we were, having to obey the whims of the manager. Maybe we just weren't used to it.

We had a FA Cup tie away against Nottingham Forest and the night before that game, I went into the dining room and ordered half a dozen escargots. I finished my meal without anything being said but, as I was making my way from the restaurant, Ron Saunders called out: 'Hey, you – come here!' Then he asked me: 'Are you trying to take the piss out of me?' I stood there, dumbfounded, then he said: 'Are you not going to answer me?' And followed up by asking: 'What is my rule about eating?'

I found words for the first time, now that I knew what he was on about and replied: 'You said we can't have prawns. I had snails'. And he rapped back: 'Aren't snails like sea food?' I gaped at him, feeling like a little boy lost, then mumbled: 'I'm … I won't do it again.' I suppose the ban on seafood was a precaution in case of food poisoning, but I confess it had never occurred to me and maybe if it had been explained in that way, it would have made more sense. But the order 'no prawn cocktails' was never accompanied by an explanation.

At that stage I had been having one of my best seasons and Johnny Hart, who was still on the staff, had told me :'You're playing as well as I've ever seen a sweeper play in this country.' I felt the job was demanding a great deal from me, but I had accepted the responsibility and that was that. But you can't win them all and when we played at Ipswich and lost by the odd goal in three, I was the man responsible for one of the Ipswich goals. Then we played Sheffield United and again I had to hold up my hand when they scored a goal. But those were the first two mistakes I had made during the season. However, Ron Saunders showed that he had spotted them, for he pulled me on one side during a training session and said: 'People have been trying to make me believe you're a good player. What's all this I've heard about you?' I was stung by his sarcasm and simply let it go by answering:

'You're the manager. You judge me as you see me.'

By then, there was no real harmony in the Maine Road camp and many of the players admitted that they were dead set against the manager. Some of them had pre-judged him; others had adopted their attitude after his arrival. It all boiled down to the same thing. Team spirit was not as good as it might have been and the focus of our dissatisfaction was the manager.

After the game against Nottingham Forest, Rodney Marsh had to go into hospital for a cartilage operation and I went to see him. For the first time in my life at Manchester City, something was sticking in my throat, as I weighed up my feelings about the club. The dressing-room atmosphere was terrible and I felt I was getting into a hopeless situation. When I saw Rodney, I told him about the manager's remarks to me and he said: 'I've never been so sick in my life.' He wasn't referring to the cartilage operation either. I said: 'I feel exactly the same. I don't even look forward to training any more.' Rodney answered: 'There must be something wrong when someone like you says that.' And he was right.

Despite all the discord and the lack of spirit in the dressing room, City managed to play their way through the various rounds of the Football League Cup and we eventually got to Wembley, where we met Wolves. We went down to our headquarters on the outskirts of London, there was no party spirit and we trained on pitches at the back of the hotel that had more slopes on them than the Alps. All we were allowed to drink was orange juice, not even a glass of wine with our meal. We felt that we were not being treated as men, but as children who might get sick at the party if they ate too much. Frankly, I don't believe any of the players were in the right frame of mind to go out and do their stuff in a Wembley final. I think we had lost that final before we even went on the park. Saunders was full of tactical talk and he did everything you would expect a manager to do, in the effort to gee us up. But there was no way we could brace ourselves so that we were in the mood to produce the goods. The aftermath of our defeat at Wembley was that Ron Saunders was on his way, even before the season had ended.

I know he had tremendous success at Aston Villa after he left City, but I believe that if he had stayed with us, we would have been in danger of going down to the Second Division that season. His departure lightened the gloom straight away. Chairman Peter Swales held a meeting with the players and asked us what we thought about the situation. Most of us admitted that there was general unhappiness, that the atmosphere had degenerated and that there was no more spirit in the dressing room. So many things had changed for the worse. For the chairman, it must have been a tricky job, as well as a distasteful one, in telling Ron Saunders the way things were.

116

Only a few months earlier, Peter Swales had listened to the players' views, then made his own decision – to employ Saunders. Now he was publicly reversing that decision, in the full knowledge that the players had finally made their point. It wasn't a determined display of player power that ousted Ron Saunders, because I am sure that if we had found him different from our expectations we could have got along pretty well, even though we had been plugging for Tony Book. I make no apology for saying that Ron didn't help himself, didn't go out of his way to be understood and didn't really give himself a chance. His sergeant major tactics may have worked at Norwich and they clearly made an impression at Aston Villa – unless he learned a thing or two from his experience at Maine Road and possibly soft-pedalled a bit, especially with the sarcasm.

What I do know is that City's chairman gained even more respect from the players because he showed that he could admit to having made a mistake. When Saunders had gone, City finally turned to Tony Book and handed him the top job.

12

SKIP

TONY BOOK
(MANCHESTER EVENING NEWS, 17TH NOVEMBER 1975)
*He is what Manchester City is all about. He will give his heart and
soul for this club.*

THERE WAS A hard core of steel inside Tony Book. He did
things his way and he was not easily deflected from his
purpose. I remember playing against him when he was with
Plymouth Argyle; he had the job of marking Mike Summerbee
and it was one of the few occasions when Mike had to admit
that his opponent hadn't given him a kick. Tony was quick and
strong and even when Mike did manage to knock the ball past
him, he had turned in a flash and whipped the ball for a throw-
in. On that performance alone, Tony Book was good enough for
me and I saw nothing strange in his arrival at Manchester City,
even though he had come into the game at league level
relatively late in life.

I had graduated through the various ranks and I had been
in professional football since I was a lad; to me, it still seems
that it must be extremely tricky for someone to make his bow
in league football well past the age of 20. There are few who
players can achieve success in that situation. Steve Heighway
did it with Liverpool and Tony Book did it with Plymouth and
Manchester City. But as a general rule, a player who is going
to make it to the top must be looking to break through to the
first team by the time he is 20.

At the age of 20, I was playing for Manchester City in a
derby game against United, before a full house of 63,000

people. Tony Book's experience, when he arrived at Maine Road as a real latecomer, had been pretty limited. Yet, after lengthy spells with Bath City and Plymouth Argyle, he was able to go straight into the City side and I know I thought of Tony and Alan Oakes as being two of the outstanding players when we had gone on from our promotion season to win the First Division championship. Malcolm Allison didn't push for City to sign Tony just because he had a remarkable turn of speed – his reading of a game was also exceptional and he was playing as sweeper in our first season in Division One. Tony's attitude was dead right – he never wanted to lose. He was a man after my own heart and while I may be biased in his favour, I always liked this quiet fellow who had enough brains to feel his way before committing himself. He was intelligent as a player and he utilised that intelligence as City's manager. I have always found Tony Book totally committed to a cause in which he believes, too. He was as dedicated a footballer as anyone I have ever seen – maybe he felt time was so short for him at the top – and I have never known anyone train harder.

Tony, who had cost Plymouth only £1,500, had played 81 out of 84 games in his first two seasons with Argyle ... and he created a good impression in his first couple of matches for the Blues.

He was 'the star in both matches ... a revelation,' said Joe Mercer, after we had beaten Liverpool in Tony's second game. By the end of his first season at the club, a new star had emerged and he received the first Player of the Year award from the City Supporters Club. In 1969, he shared with Dave Mackay, the Footballer of the Year award in the national poll.

Tony made his career stretch out until we all began to wonder if he was ageless and during his seasons as a player I cannot remember anyone giving him a chasing. There were some good wingers around, too, yet Tony could give them five yards from the half-way line to the touchline and still beat them to the ball. The only real battle he had was with Johnny Morrissey, of

Everton – they used to get stuck in around the touchline like a couple of combine harvesters. Morrissey was no mug and a hard man. He would get a whack in and Tony would say: 'One to you.' Ten minutes later, it would be Morrissey saying: 'All square.' And so the duel would go on, through 90 minutes. Each man had a great deal of respect for the other and whichever one of them got to the ball first, he knew that his opponent intended to come out on top in the next duel.

Tony's attitude as a player – he became an inspiring skipper of the side – was infectious, too, because when you could see this so-called 'old man' going hard at it right to the death, you were driven to think: 'I've got to show I can keep up with him!' In his playing days,x he helped me more than anyone else on the park. I played right in front of him then and there were times when I was probably a bit careless, as I ventured up field on one of my raids. In my eagerness to invade the opposition's penalty area, I tended to forget my own defensive duties. So when I did make a mistake, Tony would bawl me out. Afterwards, he would make it his business to have a quiet word with me and put me right. And when things were going wrong for me and I was out of the side, he was always the guy who said to me: 'Keep your chin up – you'll get back."

Tony made a tremendous impression on all the City players, because right from the start he showed that he was as dedicated a professional as any of us and it soon became clear that he had the ability to match anybody's readiness to graft. I believe he also felt he owed Malcolm Allison a debt for having given him the chance to break through to the big time as a player and during Malcolm's reign at Maine Road he had no more loyal supporter than Tony. When Mal left and Johnny Hart was handed the job, Tony gave him the same sort of backing as assistant manager. He hadn't changed one iota. Always, he did his own job, whether as player or back-room man, with a quiet air of authority and you could not help but respect him.

It must have been a fairly difficult time for Tony when he knew that we had wanted him to be 'the boss' and saw Ron Saunders arrive as manager. Yet Skip never allowed anyone to question his loyalty to the new man and, when Ron Saunders left and Tony became the Number One, he remained exactly the same. A fellow you could share a laugh and a joke with, a fellow who knew what it was like to be a player yet he was also someone who was determined to do the job his way. And we all knew and accepted this.

I don't know if Tony Book had any sleepless nights when he was finally given the job the players wanted him to have – if he did, it didn't show and he handled many problems after he took over the managerial chair. For a start, he had to get the atmosphere right again at the club, although he would probably admit that the players immediately responded to his appointment by showing that he had their wholehearted support. He had to get us going again and mould a side that was capable of winning trophies, as had been the case when he was City's skipper. He had to make decisions about the team, handle big-money buys and make some himself and erase that City reputation of being a side which seemed unable to win away from home.

When Tony was a player, you never really knew he was there. He was soccer's original Quiet Man. He never smiled or cracked a joke before a game – he would just get changed and start limbering up, putting all his concentration into the business of preparing himself, mentally and physically, for what lay ahead. I have my suspicions about one thing, although I doubt if, even now, Tony would admit it. I reckon that when we got back into the dressing room at half-time, he would sneak away for a quick smoke, just to calm his nerves before going out again.

When Tony became the manager, it might have been thought that he would suffer some uncertainties in the early days and that this would affect his ability to make quick decisions. In fact, I never noticed this at all and I think the reason was that, as assistant manager, he had already taken a fair amount of the strain at the club. Furthermore, he knew that the players had wanted him as 'the boss', so he already commanded their complete respect and he was entitled to expect their loyalty too. Everyone knew his attitude. He wanted a fair day's work for a fair day's pay and no excuses or slacking.

He always told a player that he was in or out before anyone else got to know and that hadn't always been the case at the club in years gone by. It's a terrible thing when a player picks up a newspaper and turns to the back page to learn from someone who is outside the club that he is being axed or 'rested' from the team.

I reckon that Tony Book probably lived on his nerves more when he was a manager, than he did when he was a player. I'm not sure if he still smokes cigarettes, although these days he doesn't have to nip off to the toilet for a quick 'drag' at half-time. But the tensions of the job tend to show, in little ways and when you're used to a guy you can sense how he's feeling. He was never a man to duck, when the bullets were flying.

There was a time when he decided to give up smoking. I think he'd made a New Year resolution and we all wondered just how long it would last. Along came the FA Cup and we were drawn against West Brom at Maine Road. We couldn't beat them on our own ground, so we had to travel to The Hawthorns and we got through in the replay. The FA Cup always has a special significance and it arouses passions in players and spectators alike. It must be murder for the manager in the dugout, seeing what should be done and what's going wrong, at times and being unable to do anything about it. That night, Tony had been shouting himself hoarse. In fact, he had become so involved in the game, when we got back to the dressing room, Joe Royle, a typical witty scouser grinned at him: 'For fucks sake, Skip ... get back on the fags ... I'm sick of seeing you bite lumps out of the bench!'

Tony Book treated his players sensibly, knowing that he could rely upon them to respond and react to his methods of working with them and after he became the boss, he established a great relationship with the rest of the lads. At the same time, we all knew he could not be taken for granted, or played for a sucker – and many a time he gave us a real rollicking, when he has felt we've deserved it.

I think it was Sir Matt Busby who used to say that 'if things are right at the top, they will be right throughout the club.' Whilst Tony Book was the undisputed manager of Manchester City at that time, the man right at the top was the chairman, Peter Swales. I always remember what a business rival of Swales' once said: 'He is a hell of a nice guy, but he tends to leave a few dead bodies lying around.' Certainly Peter Swales rocketed to the top of the football tree, at boardroom level, in a way that few people could have matched. He also showed that he could be ruthless when he saw the need for drastic action. Peter Swales made a lot of people wonder when he went on television and declared: 'I am the boss at Maine Road and the manager knows it,' but I can confirm that so far as team matters go, Tony Book was very much the boss.

13

THE WORLD IN MY EYES

THERE WAS ONE incident that I remember from one of our European adventures involving one of the younger lads whom, much as I'd love to, I cannot name in case it causes embarrassment to his family. All will be revealed, except his name, of course. It was just after a friendly with Ajax in Amsterdam. We'd drawn 3-3 and Johan Cruyff had scored a hat-trick. It was funny because when they got a corner they were shouting instructions to each other in Dutch. When we had a corner we'd be saying things like 'you spin off around the back' and the Dutch lads would come back with 'keep an eye on him when he spins off'! Their English was as good as ours and I suppose we were a bit naïve in retrospect.

After the match we all went out – the City and Ajax lads – for a few beers in town. One of the young lads came with us – he was only sixteen – but for a young lad he had the biggest chopper you've ever seen! I remember Oakesy asking once 'have you ever used that?' to which the young player responded that he hadn't. So we had a few drinks and ended up in the Amsterdam red light district – the Canal Strata – as it was known locally. There were five of us including the lad and we'd all decided to club together to buy him a few minutes with one of the local ladies who were displaying their wares in the windows – I'm sure you can imagine what I'm getting at.

One was absolutely gorgeous and we told the lad, 'Go on, get your self in there'. We gave him about £10 and he went in, happy as Larry. We sat over the road waiting for him and about half an hour later we starting to get worried as to where he was. Just then, a light went on in the room he entered and the lad came running out in his trousers and his shirt hanging out – no shoes or socks, mind. We all bolted wondering what had happened and as we ran the lad shouted 'Doyley! Doyley! Give us another tenner!' Any normal fellah would have lasted about five minutes but not him. If only I could reveal his identity ...

Being a footballer at a top club had many benefits and I suppose to a certain extent, that goes without saying (so why have I said it?). One of the best things for a lad like me who was raised on from a council estate, was getting to see the world and meet people you would never know but for your connections. One such person was a Greek shipping magnet who was also the owner of Olympiakos and if you glance back at some of our friendly matches played during the late sixties and early seventies, you will notice several trips to meet the Greek side. It was much more than just a pre-season warm-up – it was a social visit and one all the players enjoyed immensely.

The guy's name Golandros and he'd gotten friendly with our chairman, Albert Alexander, and it resulted in the team flying out to Greece to play these games. The first time we went we stayed in a luxurious hotel which was just outside Athens and after we played the match we were invited out to Golandros' massive home – it was like a dormer bungalow – only 300 yards long. It was huge with acre upon acre of grounds. He had enough staff to make a couple of football teams and we learned that he had bought the mountain at the back of his house – like you do – just so nobody could build homes on it and overlook him. There were no other properties anywhere close by. Inside his home, Rembrandts and Picassos hung on the wall – originals, of course – and there was two leopards that looked real from a distance and painted in gold ... real gold.

We went out onto the patio which bordered a giant

swimming pool and he'd put on a barbecue for us. There were two grills being cooked on and they both had a suckling pig being turned over the flames. Some of the lads had a swim in the pool and, after a while, I went to spend a penny with Joe Corrigan. The gent's toilets were located under the pool and the luxury continued down below. There was every kind of scent in there as well as razors, soaps, robes – you name it, it was there. We had a sneak into the ladies to see what it was like in there and it was even plusher.

It was all decked out in pink and the taps and mirrors were all in gold and every expensive perfume you could think of was lined up to use. It was unbelievable. The headwaiter or personal assistant, whatever he was, was a smashing bloke and he led a few of us down a path to a bay area where a huge yacht was moored a few hundred yards out. He invited us on board but we declined on this occasion. Even the motor launch to reach the yacht was huge. This guy then asked if we liked wine and showed us down to the cellar. The wine racks stretched into the distance and there were thousands of bottles of all vintages stacked high.

The food was magnificent and I doubt that if you had gone to the island's top restaurant that you would have got better. We were a much-sought after club back then and I travelled all over the world with the Blues and it was times such as the Greek trips that I'll never forget.

But it wasn't all fun and games in Europe and one particular memory still leaves a sour taste in my mouth. City played one game abroad against Spanish side Valencia and it is the first time I have ever seen Mike Summerbee so utterly demoralised. The left-back was built like a heavyweight boxer and he blatantly 'chinned' Buzzer in full view of the match officials and without the ball being anywhere near. All this defender did was kick Mike all night – it was an absolute disgrace. An Argentinean winger butted me, too. I'd tackled him and he was still on the floor as I got up. I knew he wasn't injured because I hadn't touched him so I went to help him up. He put out his arms and as I pulled him up he spat straight in my face and as I put my head down he butted me. I had six stitches inserted after he had split my head open. Yet nothing was said. I remember two valid claims for penalties being brushed on one side – in one case, the ball had already crossed the goal line and then a defender had scooped it out again with his hand. The referee was a proper wimp and was too scared to take any action – in fact, I think he was even wearing braces under his shirt which gives you a clue to the sort of man we were dealing with.

When you get things like this happening, it becomes easy to understand why so many British sides have come away seething after losing important ties against continental clubs. You don't mind being beaten fair and square, but you don't like it when you feel the odds have been stacked against you from the start. When Manchester City played Juventus in season 1976/77, some of the tackling – and I use the word loosely – was diabolical. There was one occasion when the Juventus goalkeeper, Dino Zoff, took a goal kick. He kicked the ball out of his hands and Dave Watson, myself and Willie Donachie stood facing the Juventus goal, ready to break up any attack that might develop from the kick. As we were preparing to go up for the ball and head it away, we found that Italian players were right with us – not worrying too much about making contact with the ball, so long as they clobbered our thighs with their boots. You were watching the ball … they were watching you. When the dust had settled, you would find that they had left their mark all right, with studs down your thigh.

The worst tackle of all was made on Tommy Booth, who was caught right between the shoulder blades with a boot. Tommy's back showed six stud marks – and Tommy stood 6ft 3in tall!

There was another time when we had to – technically – travel overseas and I can tell you it was one of the most unnerving experiences I have had to this day. The match in question was a European Cup Winners' Cup-tie with Linfield of Northern Ireland back in 1970. We played the first leg at Maine Road and just edged it against what I considered to be a non-league side. Funnily enough, we had only just managed to beat non-league Wigan Athletic 1-0 by the same score not long before so we'd been given two tough matches by teams we really ought to have been cruising home against. A neutral would have trouble telling which side was the First Division team on both occasions. Linfield battled well and deserved better, so we knew that when we travelled to Belfast we were going to be given another close game.

But it wasn't the game that was worrying me and the rest of the lads – it was Belfast and the way things were over there. It's all right reading about the 'Troubles' in Northern Ireland in the comfort of you own living room but experiencing them first hand was totally different. We arrived and drove away from the really bad areas to our hotel. The next day, however, we drove into Belfast centre. There were armoured vehicles and police cars parked up along the route and we were given a police escort normally reserved for such dignitaries as the Pope. Streets were cordoned off near the ground and the atmosphere was more than uneasy. We lost 2-1 fair and square – no excuses – but we were glad to get out of there and back home, even if we had scraped through on the away goals rule. I was frightened, end of story.

Tackling Alan Ball at Highbury in 1974, with Mickey Horswill in the
background.

That's entertainment; I give a golf lesson to Bunny Girl Kika during the charity game for Man United's Paddy Crerand at Houldsworth Golf Club. Also in the picture from left to right are Paddy, Kathy, Ian McFarlane and Jimmy Nicholl.

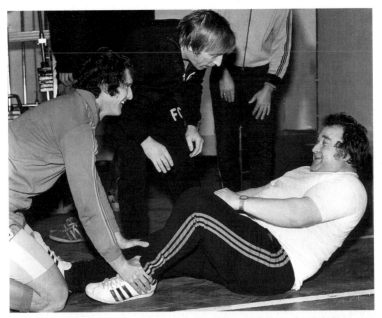

Bernard Manning regrets taking up my offer of losing a bit of weight as
Freddie Griffiths puts him through his paces.

With Little & Large and Dave Watson at Carriages.

We've done it! Final whistle blows against Newcastle in the 1976 League Cup Final. Barry Davies thought I'd suffered a heart-attack as I lay on the turf.

With the League Cup.

Outside the Town Hall for a reception in 1976.

Showing off the League Cup at the City social club with Peter Barnes and Skip.

Warming-down in the woods, near Wrexham, before
my England debut against Wales in 1976.

At Manchester Airport with England boss Don Revie.

The England connection; Joe Corrigan, Dave Watson, Dennis Tueart, Bill
Taylor, me and Joe Royle.

Living it up in LA with Kevin Keegan, Mick Channon and Phil Neal.

"It will fit you one day, son." Cheryl, Scott and Natalie with my first England jersey.

Mick Docherty, son of former United boss Tommy, joins the Blues and I show him his peg.

Me and Dave Watson welcome Kiddo in 1976.

A quiet word in the ear of young Gary Owen, about to make his debut.

Winning a header against Juventus in 1976.

There's nothing tougher than recovering from injury on your own. A hike up the Platt Lane steps in a pair of bloody climbing boots bought by Freddie Griffiths.

Soaring above the Wolves defence at Maine Road in October, 1977.

If the hat fits … with Bobby Charlton at Carriages for part of my testimonial.

With my son Scott, aged 6, enjoying a kickabout in the sunshine at Maine Road.

Scoring against Leeds United for Stoke City.

Scoring for Stoke against West Ham United.

Len Cantello measures me up for my new Bolton shirt.

My impression of an early Arthur Daley.

Scott and Charlotte's wedding day with their son Thomas and daughter Molly.

On Scott and Charlotte's wedding day with Cheryl.

14

A (Very) Brief Word on Referees

Manchester Evening News
(24th September 1968)
*It is believed that the referee has reported Doyle for an incident at
full-time when he pulled off his shirt and threw it at the referee.
Peter Baldwin, who threw the shirt back, alleges the young defender
also made a remark.*

GIVE ME ENGLISH referees every time – and I had a few brushes with the best of them but my experiences in Europe always left me longing for a home official, even if they did occasionally piss me off. I was sent off playing for City against Nottingham Forest, when the referee decided that I had made a late tackle on winger Barry Lyons. In fact, I had just managed to get my toe to the ball. I felt at the time that Barry had made the most of it, but when the referee gave me marching orders I could see that the Forest player was shocked. After the game he came up to me and told me he was sorry and that he had never imagined I would end up taking an early bath.

I received marching orders when I was playing in the United States too. I had been with the England Under-23 side on a tour to Europe and Joe Mercer had arranged for me to fly from Frankfurt to Los Angeles, where City were based at the time. I flew from Frankfurt via London and Washington, arrived safely in Los Angeles, got a few hours' sleep, and then played the following day. The game was against Oakland Clippers and we had Tony Coleman sent off after just five minutes. They had a few nationalities in their side, including a big Swede who kicked me slugged me in the stomach when we were going for the ball together from a corner kick. I turned around and smacked him one and he went down like a sack of spuds.

Okay, I wasn't going to get away with it but I was angry the referee had done nothing about the Swede punching me first. I asked if he'd seen that incident, which I'm sure he had and he said 'Why should I do anything?' Then I really lost my rag and added: 'No fucking wonder you were refereeing pub teams before you came out here.' And he had, too. He was a landlord from Barnsley and that's where he should have stayed in my opinion. Hardly surprising that I was on my way for an early bath, too. We were down to nine men with just over ten minutes gone. I'd travelled a few thousand miles to play in that match and I was back on the sidelines after just ten minutes of the action, but the was more to come. As I wandered towards the tunnel, this bloke took a swing at me – god knows who he was, but I saw it coming and laid him out. Two in a minute – not how I'd imagined things would turn out. As I went into the empty dressing rooms my studs echoed around the room. From the bath around the corner Tony Coleman shouted "Is that you, Doyley?" He must have reckoned it would only be a matter of time before I followed him down the tunnel.

He asked me what had happened and I told him, adding I'd just lamped a bloke in the tunnel. "So did I," he replied. Someone had taken a swing at TC, too and he'd punched him. If it was the same guy, he must have been the biggest mug alive, but I doubt it was. The next day we flew to Atlanta and we had an evening match there. I had been on the field only five minutes in that game when I pulled a muscle and had to limp off. It had been a long, long journey for 15 minutes' football.

Later in the tour, we were at the hotel when we saw on the news that Robert Kennedy had been assassinated. Joe Mercer later called the chairman Albert Alexander. "Bobby Kennedy's been shot, Mr Alexander," Joe said down the phone.

"Oh dear," the chairman replied. "What on earth was he doing out at that time of night anyway?" Then it clicked with Joe – the chairman thought he was talking about our own Bobby Kennedy who was on tour with us.

Back to referees and Gordon Hill was a top-class referee – even though he dropped a real clanger in a game between City and Arsenal at Highbury. Jeff Blockley was playing at centre-half for Arsenal then and there was no question about it; he handled the ball on the goal line. The sun was shining very brightly and the glare must have dazzled Hill, for he didn't award the obvious penalty and I turned in exasperation and said: 'He handled that ball out! Fucking hell!' Gordon looked me straight in the eye and answered: 'For your sake, I sincerely hope they do.'

Hill knew that football is a man's game and that there are moments when tempers can flare up. But as a player, you knew that you would have to be guilty of something really bad to get sent off. Hill applied a tremendous sense of humour to his refereeing of a game and players appreciated that they could bandy words with him – they appreciated, too, that he was quite capable of giving as good as he got, because he was a very articulate man. He was a headmaster, but he didn't look upon players as wayward children and he didn't talk down to them. He treated them as men and as equals and he expected the same sort of consideration in return.

I remember a game at Maine Road when we played Burnley and it was one of the few times I saw Colin Bell explode. Normally, Colin was poker-faced and it was difficult to know what he was thinking but, on this occasion, he rounded on Frank Casper and kicked him straight up the backside. That was out of character for Colin, so it was obvious that he must have been the one to suffer in the first place. Casper shouted to Hill: "He's just kicked me up the arse!" and Hill replied: "If you'd have done that to me I'd have kicked you in the fucking bollocks!" Play on!'

On the subject of referee's, the one I always felt had undergone a complete charisma by-pass was Clive 'The Book' Thomas. I think when he refereed in the 1978 World Cup he proved the point I'm making perfectly when he blew for half-time while the ball was crossing the line for a Brazil goal. There was uproar but only Thomas would dare do such a thing and invariably it was so he could take centre stage where he loved to be. He didn't referee another game in that World Cup as far as I'm aware ... enough said, I suppose.

My personal experiences with him were not much better and, quite honestly, one incident in particular defies belief. It was during a Manchester derby – heated games with passion and commitment all round, something you would think all good referees would take into account and maybe allow for the occasion during the odd, shall we say 'exchange, here and there. Not Clive Thomas. This was the man who could halt the mighty Brazil, let's not forget, with a peep of his whistle, but this was still four years before that game so he was just warming up!

We were playing United at Maine Road and the opinion of both sets of players (and probably fans, too) was that the match should never have taken place due to the rock hard pitch and icy conditions. But Clive thought it was okay and it was his opinion that mattered most, just the way he liked it.

About midway through the first half, I went to close down Lou Macari but slipped as I went towards him and knocked him over. It was an honest accident and nothing malicious was intended. Lou picked up the ball and pushed it into my chest and I placed it on the pitch because I knew I'd committed the foul. I ran back into our penalty area to prepare for United's free-kick but Clive Thomas had other ideas and blew his whistle, summoning me over to him. I went and stood next to

Lou and Thomas said to Macari: "You threw a punch at Doyle and Doyle responded in the same way." I asked him what he was talking about and he replied: "I'm sending you both off." Lou put his arm around me and said "Come on, we're not going off." We walked away and as we did Thomas called Martin Buchan over.

Then he shouted: The captain of Manchester City, please." I was stood a few feet away and I said to him: "I'm here. It's me." Lou insisted we were still not going off but this was one referee who would not be shoved out of the limelight and he ordered both teams off the pitch! The fans were silent as we trooped off and I can only think they thought – with good reason – the game had been abandoned.

We went into our dressing rooms – Ron Saunders was our boss then – and Clive Thomas came in and said "Right, I want both teams back on the pitch." Saunders asked if both sides would be taking eleven players out and Thomas said "No. Doyle and Macari are off." I was resigned by now that he wasn't going to change his mind. Minutes later, Lou came into our dressing room and asked what I thought. "It's fucking ridiculous," I said. I then asked Lou if he thought the game should even have been played in the first place and he said "Nah, but this is Clive Thomas we're talking about here." That summed the whole sorry episode up. I asked him what Tommy Docherty, United's manager thought about it all and he said that he was going to appeal on his behalf – and mine!

The press had a field day with Clive Thomas the following morning and rightly so. I'd been sent off before in my career but there was usually at least the merest hint of a foul or something not quite being right but nobody could fathom what had been in the ref's mind that day. I just thought Thomas was an absolute fucking big head when he was out on the pitch. All the players I'd ever spoken with seemed to feel the same way. We went to the FA for the hearing a few weeks after and we sat around a table with the officials whilst they read out the referee and linesmen's reports. Not one of them matched in their descriptions of what happened. Bert Millichip was the Chair and Tommy Docherty, who spoke for me and Lou, was fantastic in his defence of both of us. We left the room and returned to discover our fate. Millichip told us we wouldn't be receiving a three-match ban but they had imposed a £500 fine on each player – the biggest ever amount at that time. That was the end of it but, after later speaking with Bernard Halford, it seems that United paid my fine because they thought the whole situation was ridiculous as well.

Jack Taylor was another top-class referee from my day and when you look at the officials in today's game, you have to remember that most of them probably aren't anywhere near as bad as they seem – it is the over-zealous pricks at the Football Association that are making up new rules and regulations of what is and isn't considered okay. I can't recall a referee assessor sitting in the stands when I was playing. If these people were ex-professional players, I'd agree it was a good idea but they're not. The people at the FA are gradually turning football into a non-contact sport and if it had been as bad when I was playing, I'd have missed half the season in suspensions.

15

BAD BOYS

MY GREAT ESCAPE
(DAILY MIRROR, 11TH DECEMBER 1971)

*Mike Doyle, Manchester City's man of steel, last night talked about his
great escape. Doyle, who had been fouled by Ipswich Town skipper
Derek Jefferson, sprang up with his fists bunched and ran after Jefferson
who sprinted away until the City man was restrained by team-mates.*

FOOTBALLERS ARE NO angels and sometimes they present
problems to clubs just as much as they present problems to the
opposition on the field of play. Look at what has happened with
Rio Ferdinand at Old Trafford and look at what's happened at
Chelsea, Arsenal and Leeds in the not-too-distant past. Usually
the problems are easily sorted out, because they spring from an
over-exuberant display of high spirits, especially when the
pressure of the game has produced a build-up and there is a
sudden release. Players come in all shapes and sizes and their
temperaments vary greatly. In my day, there were quiet guys, like
Tony Book, while others have a jaunty bounce in their step the
moment they walk into a club.

The first time I met Tony Coleman was on a course at
Lilleshall and he would have been about 15 years old. He had
a crew-cut, seemed to have tattoo marks all over his arms,
wore jeans and a T-shirt and spoke with a Scouse accent you
could almost cut with a knife. He was on the books of
Tranmere Rovers then and you could see he was a very good
prospect. The men in charge of the course were Walter
Winterbottom and Joe Mercer and all the youngsters paid
them due respect. Only one guy didn't address either of them

as 'Mr' – right from the start, it was 'Walter' and 'Joe' to TC.

We were at Lilleshall for eight days and I remember that when he had an hour or two to spare, Tony would borrow a bike and sneak off to Newport to enjoy himself there. When the course was drawing to an end, some of the lads became a bit bored with things and decided to liven things up. There was some horseplay in one of the third-floor rooms and the next thing you knew, a bed was coming out of the window. The story went the rounds that it was Tony who started the ball rolling, to inject some excitement into what he felt was becoming a repetitive sort of existence.

The next time I met him, he had just signed for City and he joined us in time to go for a few days' break we were having at Blackpool. While we were at the seaside, we went out for a drink one night, but when we got back to the hotel, no one could find Tony Coleman. Then George Heslop appeared and said: 'Look at this.' And there was Tony, fast asleep on a Georgian-type settee, which looked as if it would cost a fortune. He had fallen asleep with a cigarette in his hand and that had burned a hole in the settee, while some vodka had also been spilled on the fabric. There was a hell of a row behind the scenes about it and when Malcolm Allison got us on the beach before training the next day, he gave us all a real roasting. 'I bring you away and this is how you carry on,' he said. Tony admitted he was the culprit – only a few of the lads had seen what had happened – and the incident was considered closed … with Malcolm cracking on that it meant taking the manageress out to a champagne dinner, to smooth her ruffled feathers.

There was another time when TC turned up at the club with an ankle twice the size it should have been and bruises all over one hand. He couldn't train and explained to Malcolm that he'd been to the baths at Southport that weekend and slipped down some steps. Mal soon rumbled that the baths weren't even open in winter and that Tony had been in a punch-up somewhere. I recall shortly after he arrived he bought a Ford Zodiac, a big monster of a car and I also had one in dark blue. TC bought one in bright yellow! Joe Mercer asked him: "Why did you get a car that colour?' You're going to get noticed all over Manchester. Get someone to tone it down." TC said: "All right, boss." He had a mate called Ken who owned a body shop in Gorton. He came the next day and his car was two-tone – yellow and purple! Joe took one look at it and put his hands over his eyes and shook his head.

Two City players had quite an experience when we were touring the US. Although we stayed in a hotel, we didn't have breakfast there – we used to go off to a restaurant a block or two away and it was while they were dining in there one morning that Neil Young and George Heslop found themselves in the middle of a stick-up. A fellow walked in, told everyone 'don't move', pulled out a gun and shot a woman in the arm. Neil and George didn't wait to see what happened after that – they were out of the door before the fellow could even wave the gun in their direction.

Youngy had a similar adventure when we stayed in Atlanta, Georgia. He heard a commotion on the corridor of the hotel and came out of his room to hear a shout of 'Hey – stop!' and there was a copper, with his gun levelled at some guy further down the corridor. Youngy felt like he was in a long-running movie – he'd seen it all before – and after that he was very wary of venturing out again.

Then there was the time Johnny Hart had to bail Tony Coleman and Stan Bowles out of jail. Apparently there had been some argument about paying a bill when they were coming out of a bar and the police were called. They didn't mess about – they hauled Tony and Stan off to the cells. A message came through to say where they were and that they could be allowed out on bail, so Johnny went down to the cooler. He reckoned afterwards he had never been so frightened in his life. As he walked down the corridor between the rows of cells, he passed drunks, drug addicts and people who looked just plain ugly. The two City players had to be right at the end of the corridor, of course, and as they walked out of their cell, one of them was carrying a shoe which he rattled against the bars of the other cells as he walked along. It was three o'clock in the morning and it was bedlam as the other inmates stuck their arms and heads through the bars, trying to grab the shoe and hollering for quiet.

I got involved in an incident when we were touring Australia, but it really wasn't of my own making, although I finished up knocking a guy down some steps. We had a couple of characters that acted as organisers and couriers for us and one of the guys was excellent. The other seemed to spend more time with his hands round a bottle than anything else. He was rarely sober and, when he got drunk, he began to get rude. We played a game in Melbourne and were up around 10 o'clock in the morning – and there was this guy, drunk while he was having his breakfast. We all went off for the match and afterwards returned around 11 o'clock at night to the hotel … to find our friend slumped in a chair, with a bottle of whisky in front of him. We were walking past him when Alan Oakes said: 'I think we'd better get him to bed.'

So we moved the whisky away and were surprised to hear him referring to us as 'Pommie bastards'. He told us in no uncertain terms to leave the whisky where it was, mumbling: 'I don't want any Pommie bastard putting me to bed.' Then he said he'd had a lot of troubles that day and was mourning the death of an aunt. I couldn't help telling him: 'You must have got through some relations during the last fortnight!' We left him then, but a few days later he had disappeared from the scene, so we reckoned Joe Mercer and Malcolm must have said something about the way he had been going on, when he was supposed to be organising things for our tour.

We moved on to Sydney and were invited to attend a press reception at which an award was being presented to an Aussie footballer. He had made a four-hour plane trip – from Adelaide, I think – to attend the function and, if memory serves me right, he had paid his own way. While I could admire that, I couldn't respect the remarks one of the speakers made about the player, for he gave the footballer a bit of a slating in our view.

Eventually the fellow sat down and by this time all the City lads were discussing the speech and not feeling in a very complimentary mood about it either. Mike Summerbee asked the fellow if he wrote for a comic paper and the guy said something in reply which I couldn't make out, except for the word 'brandy'. That seemed to be the end of the matter and shortly afterwards I nipped out to pay a visit to the toilet. I realised that the fellow had followed me and he told me: 'If you don't tell your friend to apologise, I'm going to print a story that your team demolishes a full bottle of brandy before going out to play a game. I've seen you going through the brandy like it has gone out of fashion.'

This was ridiculous and I told him: 'Nearly every player in the game has a swig of brandy before he goes out to play. It just gets the stomach warm.' But he came back at me: 'I can make you look like a team of drunkards.' I told him I would give him a hiding if he wrote such rubbish and the next thing that happened, he had started to swing a punch at me. So I moved quickly and got in the first blow ... and he fell backwards down about 15 steps. He'd even had at a go at the Queen at the table and refused to toast her, which had also pissed me off no end so I felt justified in busting his nose. He began shouting and bawling and everyone came dashing out of the room where the reception had been held. Johnny Hart was first on the scene and I thought quickly, as I said: 'Thank God you've come. You've just stopped me knocking this bloke

139

down the stairs.' Johnny gave me a funny sort of look, but there was no more trouble from my Aussie friend and we all left quietly to climb aboard the coach which was waiting to take us back to our hotel.

The postscript came a couple of days later, when we were playing the Australian national eleven in Sydney and our friend had gone into print with a story which implied that Manchester City were by no means one of the best sides to come out of Europe and that we were lucky to have won the various trophies we had collected. We made him eat his words, by winning by three clear goals and, if memory serves me right, I think I scored all three goals, which would have really pissed him off.

Incidentally, it was on the flight out to Australia that we gave Joe Mercer a bit of a shock. We travelled via Bahrain and Bangkok and at Bahrain, an Arab boarded the aircraft and sat close by Joe. Franny Lee turned to Mike Summerbee and said: 'We'll have a bit of a laugh here.' So he wrote out a note and called Johnny Hart over and asked him to give the note to Joe. Instead, after reading the note, Johnny went towards the cabin and asked to speak to the captain. The captain emerged from the cockpit and spoke with Johnny who explained they were attempting to wind Joe up and then asked if the captain would deliver it personally.

"I'll do better than that," said the captain. "I'll type it on official notepaper in the cockpit." With that, he disappeared for a few minutes then returned in full uniform carrying a neatly folded. He approached Joe and said: "Mr Mercer? This is for you." And then he walked back to the cockpit. Joe opened the note and read it. It said:

Dear Mr Mercer, please accept our apologies for not noticing earlier, but we believe the man you are sat next to be a known hijacker who is possibly armed and extremely dangerous. Please keep him talking until we land.

140

Poor Joe glanced at the man next to him. Nobody knew him from Adam and he wasn't travelling with our party so Joe reckoned this must be for real. He began chattering like there was no tomorrow and the lads all cracked up as he continued to talk as if his life depended on it, which he actually thought it did. Eventually, Franny and the rest of us couldn't keep the act going any longer ... we just had to burst out laughing and when Joe twigged that it was all a joke, he grinned back and said: 'You're a right shower of so-and-so's.' The bloke turned out to be an airline engineer who had got a 'jump-seat' to fly back to England.

There's nothing footballers enjoy more than being able to relax and let their hair down after a hard game and this usually means going out for a few drinks and knowing it doesn't matter if they get to bed in the small hours of the morning. I remember an occasion when we were in London for a testimonial game for Frank Sibley, who played for Queen's Park Rangers and naturally we stayed overnight. Some of us went out for a few beers afterwards and we called in at a few nightspots before returning at around 6 o'clock in the morning. Franny Lee, Mike Summerbee and Malcolm Allison were doing their own thing and we didn't see them at all ... until we were strolling back to the hotel as it was coming daylight and there was Franny, with what looked like a great big sack dumped over his shoulders, coming round the corner to the hotel.

It turned out that the burden he was carrying was Malcolm Allison, who had finally succumbed after a visit to a pub in Covent Garden. We escorted Franny upstairs and he reverently laid our assistant manager on the bed in his room. Big Mal was still sleeping it off as we stole away silently and headed north for Manchester. That Frank Sibley testimonial match was where one of those crazy incidents in football cropped up. Mike Summerbee never wanted to be a loser, even in a friendly and he was going straight through, with a good chance of scoring, when he was brought down inside the penalty box. No doubt about it, it should have been a spot kick, but the referee didn't award one. So Mike called him by an uncomplimentary name. Pick any one from ten and you'd be in the right area.

The referee turned and had a word with Mike in turn, then Mike said something else and we heard his next remark, which was: 'You've got to be joking!' The referee replied: 'No, I'm deadly serious.' And Mike began walking towards the tunnel. We all thought it was a case of Mike having a laugh, but once he'd started walking he didn't stop until he had disappeared from our view. The referee had sent him off, leaving us all with one thought – there was just one guy that could happen to in a testimonial match – Buzzer.

Tony Book had his problems at Maine Road when he became the boss – there was a time when it seemed we simply couldn't win a match on enemy territory and something had to be done to stop the rot. We finally cured ourselves of this ailment, but other problems developed and, as captain of the team, I shared the anxieties of the boss. That's not to say my team-mates couldn't have cared less, either – all of us had to graft and work at the job of getting our game right again.

I must admit that I had always wanted the chance to be skipper of City, although I'd not lost any sleep about it, but when I did become the captain I felt it was a privilege and an honour. I think that to a lot of players, being skipper is something of an ego trip but I don't believe that accusation could be levelled at me. Indeed, I recognise that with players such as Asa Hartford, Dave Watson and others around, the captaincy would be in safe hands elsewhere. So I just tried to get on with my job and do my best for the team. Besides, I believed a team should have 11 captains on the park, all ready to accept responsibility.

Players generally don't take long to find out – and weed

out – the hangers-on and there are plenty around, when you're in the public eye. Some of them wanted to pick a fight with you, at that – maybe it does something for their ego. It's something I've discussed with people who might be termed celebrities and told me they often found the same thing happening to them.

I'm not much good in a boxing ring with the gloves on, but I know how to look after myself in a rough-and-tumble. I'll have a go back at anyone, so I'm not really a good guy to pick on and, when the chips are down, I don't play the part of a gentleman. I don't pretend to be one, anyway.

There was a so-called City fan who will remember me well enough, because he found that borrowing money and forgetting to return it didn't pay. He fed me a story about a friend of his having been hurt in an accident in London and so I loaned him the train fare. I didn't see him for a long time and I began to make inquiries. It turned out that he was still in Manchester and eventually I discovered him selling fruit from a barrow. So I asked him about the money. He told me he had been meaning to repay me and said he would let me have it the following week. I said I wanted it there and then, or I would tip his barrow over. He didn't believe me and began to laugh, so I showed him I could be as good as my word. Then I warned him that I would be back in a short time and would expect him to have the money he owed me. I drove back to the ground and picked up Glyn Pardoe. Now Glyn wouldn't say 'boo' to a goose – but he has a swarthy complexion and from a distance could be mistaken for a tough guy.

I went back and parked the car, leaving Glyn sitting in it. I found the barrow-boy hiding in a doorway. Quietly, I told him to peep out and look at the man in the car. 'If you don't pay up now,' I told him, 'my pal is going to shoot your knee-caps off.' I'm sure Glyn hardly knows one end of a gun from the other, but the trick worked and this guy paid his debt.

I had another brush with some characters that I presume were United fans, after I had returned home injured from a game at West Ham. I had arranged to meet my wife and a couple of friends in a restaurant and, because I was late arriving, they were already waiting. Otherwise, feeling as I did, I would have skipped the evening out and gone straight home to bed. When I got there, I heard three men and three women talking and I caught the names being mentioned Tony Book, Brian Kidd and Dave Watson. For a few moments, I thought these were City supporters having a go at us because we had lost at West Ham.

As we were going in for our meal, the group obviously recognised me and I heard a chant of 'We hope you've broken your leg.' I didn't bother and went in to eat. We were seated six or seven yards away from this party and the remarks that came out were really vulgar. When we had finished our meal, as I was walking past them they began singing again and while I was sat having a drink in the bar, they came walking past me and disappeared down the stairs. Shortly afterwards they returned and the three men were limping, clearly taking the piss out of me.

So I called one of them over and he just looked at me, then stuck two fingers in the air and started singing 'We hope you broke your leg,' again. That did it. I limped over and got hold of him, then threw him to the ground, telling him to shut up and behave himself. I returned to my seat and they started again. So I went over to him and gave him a crack. Not bad for a man with only one good leg and it certainly shut him up and he most definitely had it coming to him. One of the men stood up – and apologised and that was the end of that. Except that on the Monday evening I read a story about the incident in the paper. The guy admitted that he had been taking the piss and said he had apologised, but the inference was that it had all been a bit of a joke. There was a quote from one of the women about the incident having 'completely ruined our evening'. Well, a lady likes to have the last word – and there's no answer to that.

Fortunately, such incidents were relatively rare, but they do illustrate that being in the public eye as a professional footballer can have its tricky moments. I didn't care how much folk had a go at me when I was out there on the park, but I like to be able to enjoy myself in my private life and I didn't go looking for fights. But sometimes, as I said, you cannot afford to be too much of a gentleman.

City manager Tony Book was a strict disciplinarian when it came to players behaving themselves on the field and at the start of the season he told us what he expected. He also used to warn us that we face the threat of a fine if we stepped out of line and, to my knowledge, he fined three or four players – including myself. That was after the game against Derby County and the incident with Leighton James, which ended with marching orders for me.

I had gone in for a tackle on James and, as I got up, he looked at me and I could tell he was about to spit at me. "Don't even think about it," I said to him and pushed him away. With that, he covered his face and bleated: "He's cuffed me, he's cuffed me!" I could have taken it if he'd have claimed I had punched him but he claimed it was a 'cuff'. The linesman put his flag up and the referee came over and said he'd seen me aim a punch at James and that I'd caught him in the face. "I never fucking touched him," I said, but he was adamant and, as we all know, referees don't change their minds over sending offs and he instructed me to leave the field. That wasn't the end of the matter, though. Later on, we went to Blackpool as part of a winding-down exercise meant to relax players and allow us all to let our hair down. We stayed at a hotel but headed for the disco at the nearby Savoy.

There were a few of us and I was still seething about the

incident that afternoon but I knew I had to calm down and forget about it but fate was about to play a cruel hand, depending on which way you look at it. Imagine how I felt when, Leighton James came out of a toilet just in front of us in the foyer of the disco. He saw Mike Summerbee and me and bolted into the disco and out of the emergency exit, not that it surprised me given his antics on the pitch. I can assure you, given the opportunity that night, I would indeed have 'cuffed' him but he'd disappeared into the night and ran all the way back to Derby as far as I knew or cared.

Nothing about the actual sending off was said immediately after the match but, the following day, Tony Book took me on one side and spelled it out, reminding me that he had a rule about fining players. I might be the skipper of the team, but that didn't entitle me to consider myself the exception to the rule, so I could expect to be hit where it hurt – in the pocket. The fine was a substantial one at that. I accepted what the gaffer had said and didn't grumble and there have been no hard feelings from the other City lads who had to pay up either. When something like this happens, you've got to face up to your punishment and take it on the chin.

I've been asked several times in the last few years about my view on today's so-called hard players. There are the likes of David Batty and Roy Keane but with the restrictions on tackling hard in place to such an extent that a really meaty challenge – a fair one, mind – will just as likely result in a yellow card or even red. I maintain that I would have around a dozen red cards a season if I was playing today. As I stated before, the authorities are trying to make football a non-contact sport.

That's not to say that there are those who still 'go over the top' and appear intent on injuring a fellow professional and I believe that any such offence should be dealt with severely. Take the Roy Keane tackle on Alf Inge Haaland – Keane was totally out of order and it seemed to be no more than retribution in my eyes. The tackle, as such, was a disgrace, which is a pity because I believe him to be one of the best midfielders Manchester United have ever had and one of the best in the world. He puts his heart and soul into the game as many of us used to do.

I would never have made a tackle like that, whatever the circumstances were and neither would the likes of Tommy Smith, Peter Storey or Norman Hunter who was famed for his biting tackles. I believe it was a one-off incident that went back to the time Keane was injured at Leeds and Haaland stood over him, accusing him of feigning injury. To hold that kind of anger for so long and then satisfy yourself by doing something like that is worrying, to my mind. Keane, to me, has the same attitude and application that I had when I played and in that respect, he reminds me of myself. As for glorifying the incident in his book, well that is down to the publishers who have the last shout and was no doubt included because of the controversy it would cause and as we all know, controversy means sales. To be honest, I can't understand why he wanted to write a book anyway – it's not like he needs the money.

As for the likes of Vinnie Jones, I didn't rate him at all but good luck to the lad and he's making a good living for himself now. Anyone who can be a film star as ugly as he is deserves all the praise in the world. I recall him playing for Wimbledon one time and he made a horrific tackle on a Spurs player and it was as bad as Keane's on Haaland, but he only got booked. I can't be sure, but I don't think that lad ever played again. Jones wouldn't have lasted five minutes in my day. The hard men of my day just wouldn't go over the top in a tackle – they were hard as nails, but honest with it.

16

ROLLERCOASTER RIDE

MIKE DOYLE
(MANCHESTER EVENING NEWS, 1ST MARCH 1976)

Being captain of City and being able to win the League Cup with
them is so much of a dream come true I was scared of waking up any
minute and finding out that's all it was ... just a dream.

MANCHESTER EVENING NEWS
(5TH MARCH 1974)

Once more it was Mike Doyle – who else? – that held City together
at the back to emerge as City's best player. Doyle mopped up
superbly in that first half when Wolves confidently carried the fight
to City's Cup Final veterans.

LOSING LEAGUE CUP finalists in 1974 ... League Cup winners in 1976 – add to that the 1970 victory over West Brom and the League Cup was a competition City were threatening to dominate and did, for a period. Our first victims on the way to '76 triumph were Norwich City and although we had to meet at a neutral venue – Stamford Bridge – to settle what had become a bit of a 'needle' tie, we won hands down in the end, scoring six goals to the Canaries' one. That meant that we had to play Nottingham Forest in the next round, at Maine Road.

Forest put up a plucky display and we didn't turn on a particularly good performance, but we scraped through by the odd goal in three and we couldn't have had a greater incentive to win the next round, because the opposition was Manchester United. The luck of the draw favoured us because, once again, we were on home ground but, within the first few minutes of the game starting, we were gutted about an injury to Colin Bell. He and Martin Buchan went for the ball together and when the United defender put in a high tackle, he caught Colin flush on the knee. It was an injury which was to rob City of Colin Bell's services for more than 18 months and he was never the same player again. Despite the most courageous effort to come back I have ever witnessed, his career had in effect come to a premature end.

It was obvious that Colin was in a great deal of pain as he lay writhing on the ground and, as I went over to take an anxious look, I heard him saying through clenched teeth: 'It's gone, good and proper.' He was carried off and taken to hospital, where he spent several days. Fluid had to be drained from the knee and there had been internal bleeding. The recovery process was slow and painful and close on 18 months after the initial damage Colin was back in hospital for another surgical examination, as he tried to get back into the game in time to help us on the final run-in for the First Division championship.

Colin came back and was injured again in a clash with Arsenal's Ray Kennedy. Colin slid across in front of the dug-out and Kennedy put his foot on the ball and pushed it and it seemed to open Colin's knee joint, causing even more damage. Despite the shock of the original injury to Colin at Maine Road, we were more determined than ever to see off United and we pulverised them from start to finish, scoring four goals without reply. Asa Hartford and Joe Royle got one apiece and Dennis Tueart claimed a couple of goals. So our only worry then – apart from Colin Bell – was who we would get in the next round and, again, our luck was in, because we were drawn at home against Mansfield.

However, the club from one of the lower divisions in the league played extremely well and their players never gave up on the night. It must have been an excellent game to watch and we had to keep a wary eye on Mansfield striker, Ray

Clarke, who later moved into continental football with Sparta Rotterdam. By the end, though, we had won by 4-2, taking us into the semi-finals against fellow First Division outfit Middlesbrough.

The semi finals were over two legs and the first game was away on Teeside at Ayresome Park. We had just started to run into injury problems, though. Apart from Bell, we had Kenny Clements out of action and the worst blow of all came on the afternoon of the match itself. Dave Watson had been troubled by his back for quite a while, although he had managed to keep on playing but, while we were at our hotel, his back suddenly gave up completely leaving our best defender in agony and out of the tie. In fact, Dave was lying on the floor of his room and couldn't even attempt to get mobile and we had to leave him there and collect him after the game.

Fortunately, Tommy Booth was ready to go into the side, but I began to wonder if an injury hoodoo would end our hopes of going all the way to Wembley. We had been at Ayresome Park in a League game the previous week and Boro had been lucky to score a 1-0 victory over us, so we had been optimistic about these two games figuring that if we could keep the first leg tight, we could finish them off at Maine Road. But the injury to Dave Watson had an upsetting effect upon us and we really were wondering if fate had turned against us.

As we kicked off, I was thinking that I'd be happy to accept a 1-0 defeat and as the time wore on it began to look as if we might get away without even conceding a goal. But about ten minutes before the final whistle, Boro striker John Hickson put the home side ahead and that proved to be the only goal of the game. I wasn't worried by the result and I got the feeling that we would thrash Boro when we played the return match at Maine Road.

I did a radio interview in which I made what sounded like a stupid statement – I forecast that we would stick five goals past

Jack Charlton's team when we met them again and the interviewer felt impelled to come back at me with: 'You're the eternal optimist, aren't you?' He was right, of course, because Boro had a fine defence and you couldn't really think in terms of sticking five goals past them, especially when you knew they would be tenaciously defending a single-goal lead. It would be a satisfactory performance to win 2-0 and clinch the tie. Yet something told me that we wouldn't have any trouble against them and I remained convinced of this, right up to the game.

We still couldn't field a full-strength side when Boro came to Maine Road and, in fact, the injury situation had worsened. No Colin Bell, no Dave Watson, no Tommy Booth and no Dennis Tueart. Yet the lads were raring to get out on the park and have a go. Colin Barrett had been drafted into the back-four line and Kenny Clements was playing at No. 3 with the midfield trio teenagers, Ged Keegan and Paul Power and the experienced Alan Oakes. Up front we had Joe Royle, Asa Hartford and another teenager in Peter Barnes.

Within five minutes of the start, we had drawn level on aggregate and after eleven minutes we were ahead in the tie overall, 2-1. In the second half, it was a one-horse race as we stuck two more goals past Big Jack Charlton's boys and I started wishing that we could get just another one, so that I could go on the radio afterwards and say: 'What did I tell you about scoring five?' The goals had come from Ged Keegan, Joe Royle, Peter Barnes and Alan Oakes and the youngsters in the side responded wonderfully to the demands of the occasion. The fantastic support of the City fans helped us all to raise our game as well and, when it was all over, Jack Charlton and his players were looking as sick as parrots.

The general feeling amongst the fans was that the League Cup final topped off a tremendous campaign but I reckoned that even if we'd have gone out in the semi final, the performances of the three youngsters – Keegan, Power and Barnes – had been the real highlight of the season so far. If they'd done it in a semi-final, they could do it in the First Division and, with two or three more years' experience, they would be established and seasoned campaigners. That, I felt, was a real bonus.

We had been losing a Cup match 1-0 and these youngsters had been pitched in at the deep end and they had turned up trumps. The way Ged Keegan took the first scoring chance and the way Peter Barnes knocked in our third goal was almost incredible. You would have thought that these lads had been in the side all their lives.

In my mind, the final against Newcastle was a foregone conclusion – for Manchester City. Newcastle had been involved in a marathon to knock Bolton Wanderers off the Wembley trail and if Bolton could go so near to beating them, then we could certainly go one better. What was more, I felt that Newcastle didn't really fancy their chances against us. Their manager, Gordon Lee, was talking quite a bit about the problems he was having because players were going down with flu and it seemed that Newcastle would be able to turn out only half a team at Wembley.

I'm not saying that Newcastle didn't have their problems, because of players being ill, but it gave me the added confidence that Gordon Lee felt we were the stronger side and it provided us with all the incentive we needed. You cannot afford to feel sorry for the opposition – you have to be thankful for any breaks you get, especially when a trophy is at stake. As far as I was concerned, there was only one thing that mattered: to stuff the Geordies at Wembley and win the League Cup. Professionalism has to take precedence over sentiment.

So we went into the final believing that Newcastle were half afraid of us, yet, strangely enough, in the opening ten minutes they gave no sign of having an inferiority complex as they came right at us. The midfield was where they were strongest, but gradually we began to take charge in the middle of the park. We needed the rub of the green to go on and win and that's exactly what we got.

The first break came when we were awarded a free kick on the right-hand side of the field. We had been practising a set piece for such an occasion all the previous week. I stood on the centre circle of the 18-yard box and our three biggest aerial threats – Joe Royle, Dave Watson and Alan Oakes – went to the back. The hope was that Newcastle would stick someone small on me and worry more about marking our big guys. Tommy Cassidy was the man who stood with me and he wasn't the best header of a ball in the game.

Glen Keeley, Alan Gowling and Pat Howard were marking our three big men, for that was where they perceived the danger would lie. The trick worked like a charm. Asa Hartford took the free kick and our big three moved from the far post to the near post, taking their shadows with them – while I doubled round the back. Tommy Cassidy was still with me, but I'd made a bit of room and, as the ball came over, I headed it across the face of the goal … and there was Peter Barnes, all ready and waiting to stick it into the net. I was so elated that as I raced around the pitch I wasn't shouting 'Goal!' All I could think of was that our hours of practice had paid off and I was yelling: 'It worked! It bloody worked!'

We were pacing the game nicely, at that stage, but Newcastle showed they were not quite finished when they broke through the middle. Malcolm Macdonald was on my left and it looked as if Tommy Cassidy was going to go for a shot, so I thought I would try to force him to pass the ball to Macdonald, who would have to take it on his right foot – which wasn't his best one. I achieved my objective in part, for Cassidy did push the ball to 'Supermac' who mis-hit his shot, so that the ball slipped between my legs and beat Joe Corrigan. That made it 1-1 and when we went in for the half-time talk, I half-expected Tony Book to be sweating a bit, but

153

he wasn't the slightest bit worried. He told us: 'The only way you can lose this final is by throwing it away. You've got Newcastle's measure.' So we were raring to go once more and the second half will always remain memorable, of course, for that spectacular overhead kick by Dennis Tueart that produced the winner.

We started this scoring move by building up from the back; the ball went out to Willie Donachie, on the left, then across to Tommy Booth. He hit it and the ball went to Dennis, who acrobatically cracked an overhead shot past the Newcastle goalkeeper. The spectacular manner in which Dennis scored totally demoralised Newcastle – I'm certain of that. They must have felt that if we could fashion goals like that, we could score others from more conventional moves.

They had one shot from Mickey Burns that flew two or three feet wide of an upright and that was about it. I don't think Macdonald had a shot in the second half and Joe Royle got the ball into the net for us again, only to have the goal disallowed. I have always felt that a 3-1 score would have given a truer reflection of the way the game went, but we were satisfied that we had won the League Cup. You cannot ask for much more than the trophy in your dressing room, when you've played a final.

In the last 20 minutes of the match, we were playing with such poise and precision that we were stringing ten or a dozen passes together without a Newcastle man touching the ball and there wasn't the slightest sign of tension in our team. Young Ged Keegan, playing at right back for the first time in his life, had a magnificent match. His temperament was magical. The one disappointment about the day was that during the speeches at the after-match banquet, Tony Book failed to persuade Ian MacFarlane to change his mind about leaving the Blues. The big fellow had done a good job coaching at Maine Road and he had decided, for domestic reasons, to move back to the Northeast. Tony knew that the players generally didn't want to see Ian go, but despite that late attempt to keep him, his mind was made up.

Apart from that, it was an occasion for laughter and cheers all the way round – even if I did cause a bit of a problem for a waiter at the banquet. I'm not a champagne man – one glass and I begin to get heartburn. So I drank Guinness. So did a pal of mine, who had travelled to London for the game and was a guest at the reception. I called over a waiter and asked if he could get two crates of Guinness ... and he looked horrified. 'We don't stock it in this hotel,' he said. I asked: 'If I wanted a couple of lobsters, would there be any problems?' And he answered: 'None at all, sir.' So I said: 'Right, then let's have some Guinness.'

The waiter disappeared and returned shortly afterwards with a couple of crates, which he pushed under the table. Then he leaned forward and said, confidentially: 'You do realise, sir, that this is the first time this has happened at this hotel.' There was only one thing for me to do. I opened a bottle, poured a glass of Guinness enjoyed the rest of the evening, although my memory is a little hazy of the late stages as I'm sure you can understand.

I recall a meeting with Don Revie shortly after the final and he was keen to find out about the goal I'd helped set-up for Peter Barnes. Revie had picked me for the England Under-23s and he asked: "Did you work the free kick out beforehand?' I replied that we had – Newcastle had some big lads at the back so there was no point in punting free kicks aimlessly into the box. So I relayed the whole move to Revie and he smiled and said: "Fantastic. Absolutely fantastic – we'll try it when we go to America on tour."

He told me that he'd had me watched for quite a while and wished he'd picked me sooner. "I never realised how fast you were," he said. I told him you didn't necessarily need pace as long as you could read the game but he was adamant. "You've got pace but I didn't realise how much until you chased Malcolm MacDonald in the final and took the ball off him with such ease."

I liked Don because he used to send letters and flowers to the player's wives, thanking them when their husbands had been away on international duty. We were in the States on tour and I was rooming with Joe Royle, who was still asleep in bed. There was a knock and it was Revie. I invited him in and he looked a Joe who had his backside sticking out. "What the hell's that?" he asked. I said 'It's Joe's arse, boss."

'Christ," he said, "you could park a bloody bike in that!'

It was an enjoyable tour to America and I knocked about with Kevin Keegan, Mick Channon and Phil Neal, enjoying a few nights out with them. We had an official visit to Disneyland and we were shown around the park and a small room full of computerised tape machines that ran the whole place.

There was another occasion I was with England and we were playing a World Cup qualifier in Finland. I met up with Ray Wilkins at Heathrow and Don Revie informed us that Elton John would be travelling with the England party. He was huge at that time and had some involvement with Watford so we knew he was interested in football. Elton seemed fine but his manager, John Reid, looked like a woman. He had make-up on with mascara, eye shadow the lot. Elton seemed bemused to be on a normal plane because he'd probably only ever flown in a private jet before. He looked puzzled by the airport and pretty much stuck with the England lads all the way. After the match we went to a disco and Elton came along, too. It wasn't long before he was upon stage playing an impromptu gig on the piano. Peter Taylor, who went on to manage Brighton, Leicester and Hull City joined him on stage and they sang together – and they were good too.

Elton's manager gave out a big sigh when he saw what was going on and I said 'Aren't you enjoying this?' He said, 'Enjoying it? I could have got £40,000 for him doing this'. I thought, fuck me, forty grand for singing a few songs – I wondered if I'd chosen the right profession after all!

17

LEAVING HOME

STOKE'S DOYLE TOPS POLL

Mike Doyle's consistency at the heart of Stoke City's defence this season earned him the Player of the Year Trophy at Joilees, Longton, last night. Doyle polled 33% of the supporters' votes, eight per cent more than skipper Dennis Smith with last year's winner Howard Kendall in third.

DOYLE: I'M READY FOR BOLTON CHALLENGE

Mike Doyle is ready to accept another challenge and join Bolton's fight for Second Division safety – if Stoke City reduce their £30,000 price tag on the veteran defender.

PETER SWALES HAD a lot to answer for in his dealings with Manchester City, in my opinion. Had City continued with a chairman more long the lines of Albert Alexander, who allowed the manager to get on with the job instead of interfering all the time, the Blues would have gone on to great things under Tony Book and that is something I am absolutely certain about. But it had been Swales and some of the more impressionable directors on the City board who had insisted Malcolm Allison return to the club in 1979 and, in the following years, the team I loved went into free-fall. In some ways, I'm glad I wasn't there to see the really bad times as I'd enjoyed my time at Maine Road immensely.

For most of my City career, I'd been in a successful side that rarely finished outside the top ten but the club has a lot of catching up to do to make up for the barren years between 1976 and the present day. If I'd been around at the time Mal returned, I doubt I could have stopped what was happening with the established rearguard quickly sold off and an influx of raw, unproven youngsters drafted in. No, I doubt I could have stemmed the tide but I would certainly have made my own viewpoint known. Maybe I'd have been somebody Malcolm would have wanted out, anyway.

I was about to leave Maine Road and though earlier in my career I'd said I would rather pack the game in than leave City, when the club – or Peter Swales to be more accurate – made it clear they were planning for life without Michael Doyle, I knew the day I had dreaded had finally arrived. When Stoke City made a reasonable offer to me, I realised that it was time to end my 16-year association with my boyhood team.

This was back in 1978. I'd missed much of the '77/78 season with medial knee ligament damage sustained in March 1977 at West Ham United but I was well on the way to a full recovery after a couple of months out. I returned from that injury too soon and was perhaps rushed into playing when I needed more time to fully recover. My knee wasn't right throughout the following season and I missed a lot of matches, which I feel had been avoidable. It was nice to be considered so important in the grand scheme of things but I was, unknowingly, paving the way for my own departure.

I had no idea that a 3-1 home defeat to West Bromwich Albion on April 15, 1978 would be my last game in a sky blue shirt. It wasn't a great way to sign off but I had no idea at the time that I wouldn't be able to play in front of the Kippax again and feel the incredible backing of 40,000-plus fans. I still gave my all that day, as I had always done, but in all honesty we were given a bit of a hiding by a great team of the time and I was unfortunate to have been up against Cyril Regis, who was a powerful striker with pretty much everything you could ask for in a forward.

City finished fourth and qualified for Europe again and I was looking forward to pitting my wits against some of the continent's best attacks the following season. I'd experienced several campaigns in Europe and it was an exciting addition to the domestic programme's fare. But I wasn't destined to play a part in the club's next European adventure because plans were already being drawn up for life without me.

It was around the end of May that I discovered the club were about to sign promising centre back Paul Futcher from Luton Town and I didn't need to be told that he was set to be my long-term replacement. Not that it worried me – I was 32 and had a good four years left in me at least so I was prepared to do what I'd always done and battle for my place when the time came. But Mr Swales had other ideas. I'd been at Maine Road since being a kid and never cost them a penny – apart from wages – and Swales had been talking to Howard Kendall, who was the assistant at Stoke City, about signing me. The sticking point as far as Swales was concerned was money – he wasn't about to reward my services by agreeing a reasonable fee – he wanted what, at the time, was a sizeable amount. Futcher had arrived and cost City £300,000 so no doubt the chairman was keen to recoup as much money as he could which I don't blame him for but, with my services seemingly surplus to requirements, I felt he could have paved the way for me as a thank you rather than anything else.

I spoke to Kendall and he told me City were asking £75,000, which was a bit of a shock to say the least. I'd been approached by Stoke in the early seventies when Rodney Marsh's transfer needed funding. I'd refused the move then and fought back to become captain and lift the League Cup a couple of years later. This time was different and I arranged to meet Howard Kendall and Stoke boss Alan Durban at The Swan in Knutsford to hear what they had to say. Durban told me he wanted me to sign but the fee was going to cause problems.

"Whatever you can get knocked off the £75,000 fee you can have as a signing-on fee," he said. So I went to see the gaffer Tony Book and he listened to what I had to say – as he always had done – and told me to leave it with him and he'd sort something out. Not long after, Alan Durban called me to say the deal was done and I would be joining Stoke City for around £50,000. I was grateful for Tony's help and looking forward to a new challenge. It was a tremendous wrench to leave City and I was bitterly disappointed because my knee was okay but there comes a time in your life when you know it is right to move on. Stoke were a Division Two club at that time – the old Division Two – and were a driveable distance away from my home in North Manchester.

I travelled down the following day – June 6, 1978 – and became a Stoke player. I had played my City testimonial by this time – a match against England at Maine Road but it wasn't to be the big pay-off I had hoped for! It was a case of 'just my luck' on the evening on the game when the buses came out on strike. This was at a time when many fans relied on public transport to get to the game and, knowing the way City supporters had been throughout my career, I might have expected double the gate on the night, which was around 10,000. I was grateful for everyone who'd turned out and supported me but – without being bigheaded – I know there would have been a fair few more but for that bloody bus strike.

I received a nice letter from the union convenor saying how sorry he was that the action of his members had affected my testimonial and I took it upstairs and wiped my arse on it. I'd had a fantastic testimonial committee and I felt more sorry for them after all their efforts that something like that should happen. I was asked once if I kept the shirts from that night – I'd played one half for City and one for England and the match ended 4-4 – but I didn't hold on to anything like that.

I've auctioned most of my memorabilia at Christies because it doesn't mean that much to me.

All my medals have gone, too. What's the use in keeping something that is locked away in a cupboard. It's not like I took them out every day to look at them with a big smile on my face. Besides, the cash came in handy! Some people may think differently and many old players do keep their medals, shirts and other mementos and that's up to them. It's just not me. I have my memories and I cherish them as much as any tankard or sweaty shirt I've been given.

Anyway, I digress. Back to Stoke City and the reason I was happy to join them. Howard Kendall was a man I admired a lot and had got to know throughout my career. We'd been out a lot socially and had a few good sessions in Southport and I really liked the bloke. When I met him and Alan Durban in Knutsford we all got on well and I felt comfortable about everything. Believe me, I wasn't just jumping at the first offer that came along, it just so happened that the first offer was a good one. Durban told me that he wanted me to organise the defence and stabilise what he already had because the season after the one coming up they were going to have a good push at promotion.

He'd signed Ray Evans from Spurs and he had a good goalkeeper called Roger Jones and there were players such as Dennis Smith who would be my defensive partner, Alan Dodd, Terry Conroy, Sammy Irvine, Adrian Heath Garth Crooks and Lee Chapman – the latter trio all being exciting talent at the start of their careers. Alan Durban's undoing would be the fact we won promotion at the first attempt and the consolidation season that he'd planned for didn't happen.

We finished runners-up to Crystal Palace who were then managed by Terry Venables and the truth was we simply weren't prepared for the top flight. We held our own in the First Division and had a good run at Easter and a good last few games and I think we finished about fourteenth. I returned to Maine Road for the first time as a member of the opposition on Boxing Day, 1979, and received a fantastic reception from the City supporters – you don't forget things like that and I know they realised I was one of their own, even if I was representing Stoke. I was totally committed to helping Stoke win but I had blue blood running through my veins and it was an emotional day for me.

Fortunately, it was honours even so I didn't feel I'd let anyone down. We drew 1-1 that day in front of 36,286 fans. There were only five players in the City team left from my time with the club and this was only 18 months later. In fact, that draw was the start of a run of sixteen games without a win for the Blues that stretched to the return game at the Victoria Ground where they ground out a 0-0 draw. Only three wins from the last four games ensured they didn't go down. The club were in disarray and, as a City supporter, it was hard to stomach.

I can honestly say I loved every minute of my time at the Victoria Ground. We had a great bunch of lads there. There was a great team spirit and they were making the best of what we had, perhaps over-achieving if anything. Young Garth Crooks had caught the eye of Tottenham and it wouldn't be long before he was off to London to form a terrific partnership with Steve Archibald.

There was one occasion when Howard Kendall came up to me and said: "When you see the boss, just say 'You're losing your tan, boss." I asked if he was taking the piss. "No, honestly," he insisted. "Just say you think his tan is wearing off and leave it at that." I knew there was some mischievous plan behind it but I didn't mind a bit of leg-pulling so on my way out of the ground, Alan Durban passed me on the stairs.

"All right, boss?" I said.

"Not bad, Tommy," he replied.

I looked at him and paused before saying: "See you're losing your tan, there, boss."

"I'm not, am I?" he asked, looking genuinely concerned.

"Yeah," I said. "You're definitely looking a bit pale."

"Right," he said walking on, "I'll get that sorted." And off he went.

The next day I arrived at the ground and all the lads were smiling at me. They obviously knew something I didn't and it was soon after I discovered he'd booked a holiday in Majorca for all the lads! Alan Durban was clearly a man who took his tan seriously and I'm just thankful there were no sun beds around at the time!

We left a few days later and arrived at Palma airport ready for a week of relaxation, sun and boozing. We got on the coach to the hotel and two of the lads, Sammy Irvine and big Brendan O'Callaghan took their bags on the bus with them and began to get changed ready for a bender. Sammy stood about 5'8 and Brendan was around 6'4 so they were your archetypal Little and Large and they looked typical Brits abroad when they both put white shirts, white shorts, black socks and trainers on. You can imagine the colour of their legs were white as snow, as well. The residents of Majorca didn't know what was about to hit them.

At the hotel, Sammy and Brendan dumped their bags in the reception and walked out of the hotel ready for a major drinking session. Everyone else ambled in to unpack and take it easy but Little and Large were not seen again until the following afternoon. They were out until 4am in the morning and they were totally wrecked when they came back. They went to the reception and demanded to know their room number so they could get their heads down. Brendan muttered his and Sammy's name in garbled English but they could hardly stand up, let alone talk. They continued to ask for their room until the staff could understand them. Brendan, a big powerful lad was losing his rag by this time, especially when the lads were told there was no room reserved in those names. His attempts at communication exhausted and his head spinning like a Wurlitzer, Brendan reached over, picked the bloke up and said: "Get me the fucking keys, now!" The poor guy must have been quaking in his boots.

The manager appeared and threatened to call the police. Sammy tried to reason with him: "Look, we are from Stoke City – an English football team and we've just arrived last night," he slurred.

Then a light seemed to come on in the manager's head. "Oh, Stoke City?" he said at last. "Yes, you are the hotel further down the road!" Not only had they managed to abuse the hotel staff in the early hours of their first day on the island, they had gone to a completely different hotel. We had a good time in Majorca and a great laugh. There was one time Garth Crooks decided to have a go at being pulled by a speedboat with a parachute on and, to this day, it remains one of the funniest things I've ever seen. Garth put the relevant equipment on midway down this wooden jetty by the sea. He got the signal from the driver of the boat to begin the required running start as the boat pulled away. But halfway down he tripped up and was dragged about 30 yards along the jetty, banging his knees as he rolled along like tumbleweed for several painful seconds before he sailed into the air rubbing his knees and shins frantically. Howard Kendall and myself were in tears watching him. It is hard to forget sights like that and every time I see him interviewing somebody on the BBC, I just think of him bouncing along that wooden jetty.

We returned home refreshed and recharged with the gaffer's tan topped up accordingly. We did the double over City that season (1980/81) beating them 2-1 at Maine Road and 2-1 at the Victoria Ground. They were stabilising a bit under John Bond and were on their way to the Centenary FA

Cup Final against Spurs where they would face my old mate Garth Crooks.

We had another trip abroad during my second season – and not long after the Majorca jaunt – a week in Greece. We stayed at Aghios Nikolaos in Crete and played a friendly in Heraklion, all on the back of another comment about the manager's tan! He was a good lad, Alan, and he went on to do a good job at Shrewsbury Town in 1981, too. Later he moved to Sunderland but I'm convinced he was conned into the job in the Northeast.

Howard had moved into management at Blackburn Rovers and things were changing at Stoke. The new manager during what was my third season there was Richie Barker and I can say, hand on heart, that he was absolutely bloody useless. We went from a fair football-playing side to a hoofing team with instructions to 'find big Brendan' at every opportunity. He was the worst manager I've ever played under – how he ever got a job in management I'll never know.

City beat us 3-1 at the Victoria in September 1981, with Trevor Francis making his debut for the Blues. I think City must have brought around 10,000 fans with them because I'd never seen the old ground so packed. It was just one of many spiritless defeats under the new man and it got so bad under Barker that I was preparing to pack the game in. I told Richie to his face my feelings of how things were going and how little I and the other players enjoyed his tactics and he was somewhat stuck for a reply. I wonder why ...

George Mulhall, manager of Bolton Wanderers contacted me and I moved to Burnden Park before the end of the campaign. My contract with Stoke was up anyway and I think they were happy to see my wage trimmed off the bill so the move suited all parties and I was granted a free transfer. I was 32 and I wondered exactly what was in store for me in the coming years. Mulhall wanted me to do a similar job at Bolton as I'd done at Stoke – basically organise the defence and use my experience to benefit some of the younger players. Wanderers were struggling at the time but I couldn't understand why. They had some good players such as Paul Jones, Steve Whitworth, Jim McDonough and Peter Reid. They had four internationals in the side and had no right to be second from the bottom of Division Two.

My first game for Bolton was at Oldham Athletic and it was blowing an icy gale as ever at Boundary Park. A long ball came bouncing to me and I flicked it backwards to our goalkeeper but it caught the wind and sailed into the top corner at about 30 mph! I thought to myself, "Fucking hell! What a start!" We ended up taking a point and moved up a position. The next match was against Barnsley, who were top at the time (and would later knock City out of the League Cup), and we beat them 2-0 and went on a run that saw us eventually safe from the drop.

Mulhall decided at the end of the season to take us to Nigeria and I thought to myself, "Fuck me. Nigeria – again." I'd been there with City and hated every minute of the oppressive heat and disorganisation. What was the attraction with that country? We were playing the Eagles, which was basically their national team and after another internal flight we arrived at the Eagles' ground. It was packed with about 40,000 fans and it was scorching hot. I doubt any of the lads really fancied the game but players are the last to be consulted on occasions such as this. So the game kicked-off and Peter Reid played a ball out wide and I heard a loud thud as he did so. At first I thought something big had been thrown on the dusty, rock-hard pitch by the crowd but it transpired that locals had moved the ground about 40 yards sideways but left the cement stanchions of the stand in the ground! They were barely covered by grass and there was about a dozen scattered around the pitch, but you didn't know here they were until you clattered into one. What a nightmare and I can honestly say that if I never step in Nigeria again it will because the plane I've been flying on has been hijacked.

Mulhall was a smashing bloke, very knowledgeable about the game but he left Wanderers the next season and was replaced by John McGovern. We all thought it was a good move for the club because he had played under Brian Clough for most of his career and would surely bring some fresh new ideas for the team. How wrong that theory proved. McGovern had the personality of a door and was so boring to listen to that I had trouble keeping my eyes open as he droned on. Not that it really bothered me that much – I'd done my ligament again, had a cartilage out and decided to quit Bolton. I was half-wondering whether to retire or not when Jimmy Greenhoff, the former Manchester United striker called me to join him at Rochdale and I agreed to go to Spotland.

It was the worst decision of my career.

I should have packed the game in whilst I had the chance but I went to Dale and ended up with a spur in my heel – the feeling is the equivalent of having a drawing pin stuck deep inside your heel. A spur is a splinter of bone that calcifies and is absolute agony, trust me. I didn't play that often but Jimmy was a misery anyway. He brought his brother Brian in as a director of football or something but I'd had enough and retired from the game. It had been a mistake and I should have retired at Bolton. It was perhaps not the dignified end to what had been a most enjoyable way of earning my living but sometimes the heart drives you on and ignores what the rest of your body is telling you. I bet there's a large number of five-a-side players who are reaching a certain age and know they shouldn't really play anymore but the will is strong and if you love playing football, hanging up your boots is never going to be an easy decision.

I was living in Grasscroft, near Saddleworth, at the time

and I began jogging when my heel eased a little to keep myself fit. The last thing I wanted was to bloat out and pile the pounds on like a lot of former players do when they've finished. I used to meet socially with a bloke who lived near by called David Riley who was a director at Oldham Athletic. He asked me one evening if I would be interested in managing the Latics. I said I would and he told me to write and apply to the club secretary, who phoned me and arranged a meeting with the board. Cherie drove me down and dropped me outside the main entrance. There was a big Rolls Royce parked outside with an old bloke asleep behind the wheel. He was wearing one of those old pullovers that grandmothers liked to knit but I hadn't a clue who he was.

The secretary took me into the boardroom and the directors sat there looking at their watches. A few minutes later the old bloke from the Rolls Royce ambles in – my first meeting with the chairman of Oldham Athletic FC! He sat down and after a brief chitchat about general things, he asked me what coaching badges I had.

"The same as Bill Nicholson, Bertie Mee, Bill Shankly, Brian Clough and Matt Busby have," I told him.

"Have you?" he said, impressed. "What are they?"

"Nothing. I haven't any, just like the men I've just mentioned." Two or three of directors started laughing and the chairman nodded a long. "I've got experience," I added, "and that's what counts in this game."

"Oh, right," said the old man. "Well, thanks for coming along and we'll be in touch in due course."

It hadn't been the longest interview in the world and I wasn't sure if that was a good or bad thing. I left the room and the secretary came with me. "We've only had one other applicant," he told me. "It's John Wilde and he's stuck in Vancouver so we'll let you know as soon as possible."

A few days passed, then a week, then a fortnight and I still hadn't heard from Oldham until I bought the Manchester Evening News to read the headlines on the back: 'Joe Royle is Oldham's New Boss'.

I never got a letter from Oldham and I decided there and then that I was turning my back on football for good. If that's how the game was played, I didn't want any part of it. Now I was facing up to life without football and an uncertain future.

18

SNAKES & LADDERS

I WAS HAVING A BREAK from all sport and as far as I was concerned, it was an indefinite. Football was over and I had to explore other avenues of earning a living. I hadn't left the game with a fat bank balance and I had to think of ways of keeping the pennies trickling in. With four kids to feed, any savings we had would soon dwindle away without any other sources of income. During the immediate period after the Oldham Athletic shambles, I thought 'Christ Almighty, I've been in the game for more than twenty years and played just short of a thousand games and after three broken noses, broken jaws and god knows what else, it's time for a rest'. I must admit, I would have loved to have given management a crack and Oldham would have been the ideal place to start off. I'll never know if I could have cut it as the man at the top, which is one of the few regrets I have about my career.

Whatever came my way that I deemed interesting propositions, I would think about. A chap who was an insurance broker approached me and we got talking and he basically wanted me to sell his products, which included the likes of Norwich Union, Sun Alliance and other major insurers. I proposed an idea that was borne from my own experience as a player. When I was playing I had taken out a professional footballer's pension that matured when I was 35 years old. I suggested I should target footballers with no pension to offer them a similar scheme. He liked the idea and told me to work under my own steam.

I thought that the best thing to do was to visit the lower league clubs because it made sense to offer players who would need a source of income when their careers ended. I visited Bury, Carlisle, Crewe, Oldham, Rochdale and various other northern league clubs and it worked out quite successfully all round. The managers I visited to suggest the idea of chatting with their players were all very supportive and said 'no problem'. I remember starting Peter Beardsley off on a pension whilst he was at Carlisle and it was costing him just £5 a week! I was very pleased about the respect I got from the managers who would bring players in on their days off to chat with me.

But it eventually turned out a little sour.

The guy I was involved with who ran the insurance brokers invited me out to Lanzarote where we ended up buying some property. It turned out to be a bad move for me. This guy had a partner who was an accountant – something I didn't know anything about – and he said that if I wanted to continue in the business I would have to fork out £40,000. It ultimately ended with myself and this other guy having to sell our apartments to clear a huge debt that had been steadily growing.

I'd known this bloke for years yet he spread rumours of me being a waste of space and a dead weight despite all my efforts with the insurance policies. He was more than just a back-stabber because I'd worked hard for him and got no thanks. It was like football and life in general in that you never knew what was going to happen next but, for me, it was the start of a depressing period for me that, in truth, I've yet to fully come out of.

Another blow around this time concerned my eldest son, Scott. I love all my kids and I'm very proud of each of them. My first-born, Natalie, plays no part in our family at the time of writing. Sadly we've fallen out to such a degree that I think it would be hard to patch things up. My youngest daughter Stephanie is as staunch a Blue as I ever was and she's doing well and Grant, my other lad is doing fantastically well in his work and golf. Scott is another success story but there was a time when I think both he and I believed he would follow in my footsteps.

I used to take him down to training with me every now and then as a few of the lads did. He enjoyed himself and loved City as much as any youngster could. He kept a scrapbook of everything I ever did and no father could ask for more than his son to be proud of what his old man did for a living. He was doing well and was a real prospect up to around the age of 14 or 15 when we discovered he had a severe back problem. One of his vertebrae hadn't developed properly and that was his football career effectively finished. To say I was gutted would be a huge understatement because he was doing really well playing for Ashton and Tameside. The orthopaedic surgeon informed us that there was nothing they could do until he'd stopped growing and then it would mean taking bone grafts from his hips and fusing them into his discs. He never had the operation – which incidentally Dave Watson and Ged Keegan both had – and he had to wear a back support to keep his posture right. He got over the disappointment and became a good golfer and was assistant at Didsbury and is doing well with his business interests. I'll speak more about my family shortly.

So while the dodgy property deal soured me towards any post-football 'opportunities' that came my way, I wanted to keep working – I had no choice, really – and that's when I took on a job as a salesman at Atlas Trading. That job took me up and down the country and, a couple of years, later I was offered a similar position with Slazenger selling golf equipment and that lasted for about ten years. I enjoyed it thoroughly and made some great friends.

I was looking after the North West of England from Carlisle all the way down to St David's in South Wales. I knew most of the professionals personally and I visited the top courses such as Royal Birkdale, Lytham St Anne's and many others. I would meet the club pros over a pint in the pub and it was so enjoyable I never considered it as a job. It just felt like I was being paid to go and visit friends around the country. There was no hard-sell and, after a few jars, the guy I was dealing would say 'Right, what have you got for me?' The goods practically sold themselves.

It was a fantastic company to work run by two terrific blokes – Peter Witcherly who was the MD and Barry Meehan who was the sales director – and I can't speak highly enough of them, but good things can't last forever. Peter retired and Barry died within a short space of time and a guy called Mike Trethewick took over. He had been a MD at Rank Hovis MacDougall and he should have stayed in the bread making business because, in my opinion, the man was an absolute idiot. Another bloke called Phillip Jansen came in – he was 23 and fresh from university – and under their 'leadership' things went from bad to worse. Neither seemed to know one golf club from another – not a good sign when that's the business you're trading in.

Within twelve months, sixteen of the nineteen-strong sales force had resigned and I was amongst them, turning self-employed to try and continue the business I had built up over the years. I had a few customers but I was never going to get rich from my dealings, especially when countless golf businesses seemed to be going to the wall leaving stock that needed to be sold quickly and cheaply and I just couldn't compete with what was happening. It became really hard work and, rather than approach somebody who I'd known for maybe thirty years and casually sell stuff, I was forced to become competitive and try and ensure a sale and I didn't like it one bit. It was no longer financially viable for me to compete with lads turning up in a van selling bankrupt goods for virtually nothing so I decided to pack it in and go into a kind of retirement and I've not done much since.

I thought, I'm in my fifties now – what the fuck am I doing

chasing my tail? I planned to spend most of my time playing golf and walking the dogs until that hammer blow from the doctor informing me I couldn't to play any longer. In truth, I was in too much pain when I played and couldn't carry on anyway. It still sickened me to my stomach to have confirmed what I half-knew. You read about the likes of Paul Merson and Tony Adams and I can understand how easy it is to turn to alcohol when things get too much. No, golf was unthinkable and it left me wondering about my future. I loved the game and this was the time I should have been able to enjoy it the most but my football career had finally caught up on me and I couldn't take it. I have sympathy with Merson and Adams.

I still went along to see the Blues from time to time during this period. My youngest daughter Stephanie is a mad City fan and she makes sure I go along to as many games as possible. The club have had so many ups and downs since I left that the off-field problems they've had are hardly worth going over, given they are well documented elsewhere. I had a tough year in 1991 when my dad Tommy passed away. He was a great man and a big influence on my career and it was a painful time for everyone. Cherie's dad Arthur, my business partner from my days at Hartshead Garage had died a year earlier and my old boss Joe Mercer also died in 1991 – on his birthday, of all days. It was good to see so many old faces at Joe's funeral at Hoylake. I had the pleasure of playing golf with him many times at the course that backed on to his home in the years following his retirement and he was the same loveable old father-figure right up until the end. His wife Norah still attends many City functions and is a lovely lady who has kept Joe's spirit alive with her memories of him. I saw her at the Southampton game last May and she looked very well.

Peter Swales finally gave up as chairman, probably about fifteen years later than he should have, and my old mate Francis Lee became chairman. I have to say that I had no time for Swales in the end and harsh as it may sound, I couldn't have give two hoots when he passed away in 1996. I recall City playing Liverpool when his death was announced and a minute's silence observed. Ironically, City were then relegated later that same day – perhaps in memory of the old chairman who presided over more relegations than any chairman before him. As for his successor, I think Franny had the ammunition to do well and also had a great love for the club and I was hoping he would be successful and turn the club's fortunes around. I believed he would make City like they used to be and have a similar atmosphere to when we played together at Maine Road. I don't know what the ins and outs are of why he ultimately left and, to be honest, I don't particularly want to know. He had a clever enough head on his shoulders to know when things weren't going right and fair play to him for at least trying his best.

At this moment in time, I'm a bit down about a number of things but the biggest blow to my quality of life was being told I wouldn't be able to play golf again. Golf had become a passion for me since retiring (and was during my playing days, too, if truth be told) and it was ironic that injuries sustained during my football career have put paid to my participation in a sport I have almost an equal passion for. If it wasn't for my two dogs, Tigan and Rosie, I wouldn't get out much these days except maybe for a pint or two down at my local – either that or helping Grant renovate his new house. I love my dogs and they've helped me through the darkest period of my life. I take them on the golf course and have a chat with the green-keepers and they give me all the love and support I need – the dogs, not the green-keepers, that is! I know they'll never let me down.

Still, when Mr Azizi, my surgeon, told me I'd never play golf again I just turned to the bottle. I'd always enjoyed a drink but this was the start of a period that I have little memory of. That was two years ago and the effects my dinking had on my family life were devastating. My wife left me because I was constantly pissed and I was consuming a bottle of spirits a day and had my youngest son Grant not stuck by me, I doubt I'd be here today. I was heading for oblivion and I'm not proud to say that.

I was so drunk I didn't even realise Cheryl had bought a house not 200 yards away – not exactly something you wouldn't notice if you had your wits about you, I'm sure you'd agree. I have to hold my hands up and admit I was drinking a litre of whisky, rum, vodka or gin a day. I didn't care so long as it made me feel better. My saving grace was Grant who was still living with me. He said to me one day "I've stuck up for you dad and if you don't stop drinking, you'll kill yourself. The alternative is if you don't stop drinking, I'll kill you."

I could see by the look in his eyes that he meant every word and it was better than going to Alcoholics Anonymous because I love him to bits and he stuck by me when I needed him most. He reminds me of what I've done and I can't say any more. He's the reason I've pulled through this awful time when I stopped being the man I used to be but I know I'm slowly returning to my old self again.

There are a lot of people who are a damned sight more famous than I've ever been who have been through the same situation but, at the end of the day, you find people out when the chips are down. You find people who want to use you and the only work I'm involved with these days is charity – purely and simply because the people who ask me to help are doing it for a good reason. As soon as somebody comes up to me now and tells me I can make a couple of grand here and there in various schemes, I just tell them to fuck off.

I've always kept myself low key – okay, I had all that hullabaloo about hating United – which was true, but I was like Glyn Pardoe and Alan Oakes – I always classed myself in that category with those lads in so much I used to like to come home, have a pint in the pub and a game of dominos and that was that – I was happy.

I was married when I was 20 and, fortunately, we are back together again after two years apart and I can't blame my wife at all for leaving me and have to admit she was fully justified in her actions. When my mother-in-law died, she left Cherie some money that enabled her to buy her own house and get away from me. If that hadn't happened, she would have almost certainly divorced me and Christ knows what would have happened then.

Grant saved me, no doubt about that. He's a clever lad and an independent person. Ironically, he isn't interested in football and wants to be a professional golfer which he soon will be. The funny thing is, he gets on well with Nobby Stiles, Denis Law, and Tony Dunne who are all members at Northenden Golf Club where he works. Franny Lee goes there, too, occasionally and, of course, they are all former players from my day. I couldn't be prouder of him, if truth be told.

With my own golf career in tatters the doctor hardly helped when he told me I would be fine if I was left-handed. I can't have an operation on my knee because, at 55 years of age, I'm deemed to be 'too young'. I chuckled when they told me that. Apparently, the knees are worse than the hips when it comes to wear and tear because they take more weight. I'm in constant pain but it's something I've become used to. It's worse than toothache and it's because of the injuries I had as a player. I broke my kneecap and have had three medial ligament tears and an external ligament tear and a cartilage out – all on my right knee.

The severe pain started about five years ago and I thought 'what have I done'. Then I realised it was just down to the knocks I'd had. The specialist I went to see x-rayed both knees and showed me the plates and even I could see the difference between my right and left knees. The right will lock of its own accord and creaks like a wooden door and it's been difficult to sleep at night. I wish I could have the operation tomorrow but there's no chance. They reckon a new knee lasts about four years on average, though my doctor tells me there is a new material for knee replacements now but it won't be available until it has been properly assessed – maybe I should have volunteered to see if it worked!

I can cope and I get around okay but I walk as much as I possibly can. My surgeon recommended I walk to keep to keep the muscles around my knee strong because they are the only thing that supports my knee. The ligament has all gone and though it's not painful to touch I always have this dull ache. My two visits a year to the specialist invariably end the same way, with him telling me there's no change on last time, which is fine by me. As long as there is muscle tone and no further deterioration, I can soldier on. I must do ten miles a day with the dogs but I enjoy every minute of it.

Looking back, I didn't just become alcoholic overnight. I can remember a lot of arguments with Cherie because of my drinking and I've had affairs in the past, all of which ended with the marriage breaking up. Grant helped me regain my dignity and Cheryl took me back but my son Scott and daughters Stephanie and Natalie effectively disowned me during that time. It was a couple of years ago that I split with my wife and I hit rock bottom and, believe me, I was as low as I could possibly go.

As I stated before, Grant's warning was the wake-up call I needed and once I'd reunited with Cherie, Stephanie and Scott accepted the situation and are happy but Natalie and I don't speak to each other. I've not seen her for a long time and she's deprived her two daughters of her grandparents. I can understand and accept that as far as I'm concerned but I find it hard to forgive her for what she has done to Cherie. Simple as that.

19

BEING MIKE DOYLE

MIKE DOYLE
(MANCHESTER EVENING NEWS, 8TH APRIL 1972)
I am still a true Blue at heart and
Manchester City remains my life.

MIKE DOYLE
(WEEKLY NEWS, 27TH JANUARY 1973)
There is nobody who will outrun or outwork me
when I'm in the team.

THERE HAVE BEEN many things said about me in the past and apparently I have fathered another three children, which is news to me. If that's the case, I am still awaiting a maintenance bill. It's just something I have to put up with. I've had affairs and my wife has even caught me in the car with another woman. I'm not proud of it but it's happened and I've put it all in the past. I've been the target of petty jealousy from all manner of people, just as I had adulation and respect in my football career but one of the worst incidents involved my local golf club in Ashton.

There was a two-day competition and Grant played with me on the first day and we both came back with half-decent scores. Grant was a gifted young golfer and even at fifteen he was the best at the club by a mile and had represented his county by that time. The second day, we arrived early at the club and we cleared it with the club professional that we could out first because it was my first grandchild's first birthday party in the afternoon. We went out and came back and set off to help with the party. Later that afternoon, I called the club to see who had won and was told Grant had.

We went back to the club later in the day and there was a bit of a fuss about us going out early, despite it all being cleared and above board. The president of the club informed me there'd be no problem and that the result would stand but, minutes later, Grant overheard the president muttering 'disqualify the bastards!' Sure enough, we were disqualified. The president then came up to Grant and said 'Don't worry there's always next time'. Grant responded with 'You can shove your drink up your arse!' Kids eh?

Grant was banned for a month and then received a further three-month ban and we haven't been back since. They are all ten-bob millionaires who are fuelled by jealousy and pettiness and an unhealthy dislike of my son and his talents. They were backstabbing no-marks with no lives of any substance. That's the flip side of being Michael Doyle, the ex-City player, I suppose.

I go to see the Blues whenever I can or watch them down at the pub. I've never distanced myself from the club but I believe if you are always there, you get pegged as a hanger-on, something I've never been. I don't want to throw myself at City but I'm there if they need me for an ex-player's evening or charity work. The new stadium is absolutely magnificent and the best in the Premiership by far.

I miss Maine Road, like everyone else and it was great to be there for the final game against Southampton. I spent half of my life there so it is to be expected, I suppose. I got a great reception when I walked on to the pitch and it brought back a lot of memories. A couple of mates reckoned I'd got the loudest cheer of the old players but I'm not sure about that. It took me 40 minutes to walk around the pitch after I'd signed autographs and had pictures taken. I watched the game but midway through the second half, I called my son on his mobile and said "I'm a celebrity; get me fucking out of here!" It was an awful game and I'd seen enough. I wanted to remember the great days and games, not a tepid defeat to Southampton. It's a pity that one of the memories I will take from that day was Colin Bell coming out on his own instead of with the other old players before the game. I know he no longer has anything to do with Francis Lee and I have no idea what has happened between them but to think of the relationship they used to have and all the games they played together for City and England, it's a shame that they are loggerheads with each other so many years after retiring from the game.

I don't see many of my old team-mates very often except for the old reunions and supporters club meetings that are occasionally arranged. I'm glad to say Glyn Pardoe, my best buddy from my playing days has remained a great friend all these years and a couple of years ago I became the father-in-law to his daughter Charlotte, who married my eldest son Scott. They've had a little boy, Thomas, who is now 4 and I couldn't be happier for them. They make a great couple and were childhood sweethearts – Charlotte was Scott's first girlfriend. They both went their separate ways as they grew up but eventually got back together bonding the Doyle and Pardoe families forever.

We have all come out of this nightmare period stronger and closer as a family but I'm in no doubt that because of who I am and what I've done in the past that things have been much tougher for us all. It could have all turned disastrous but we've survived the storm and stuck two fingers up at the petty bastards who would have taken great delight in seeing me destroy myself. If some of the hassle was caused by career as a footballer then I regret that but, as for playing for Manchester City and being part of the club's greatest ever period, given a chance to do it all again, I wouldn't change a thing. My family have all had a lot to put up with these last few years but I'm immensely proud of them all and hopefully we've turned the corner together and can look forward to a much brighter future. I intend to look after some property my family owns in Spain in the near future and I know Cherie would happily move out there. We all love the weather and lifestyle, so maybe half the year over there and half in England would suit us, but we'll have to wait and see how things go. If anyone is wondering, I still hate United as much as I ever did but you've probably guessed as much anyway.

From now on I'm going to take one day at a time but wherever I end up, my blood will always run blue. I wouldn't have it any other way.

20

RIGHT HERE, RIGHT NOW
THE LAST THREE YEARS

Blue Blood hit the shelves in February 2003 and I couldn't have been happier with the coverage and reaction it caused. My original autobiography *My Team* came out in the 1970s and didn't cause too much of a stir but *Blue Blood* was just the opposite. I couldn't swear in the first edition but things have changed a lot since then and I was able to say things exactly how I wanted to this time around.

It received many excellent reviews and was covered in all the major newspapers and resulted in my appearances on several TV and radio programmes as well as numerous interviews with tabloid papers, particularly leading up to derby matches – in fact, it was just like the old days! I was also pleased that nobody gave me or the book a good slagging off – not even Marshy! I gave it straight in the interviews, as I've always done.

The turnouts at the 20-odd supporters club tour we did to promote the book astounded me because Mike Doyle was never a Colin Bell or a Mike Summerbee – that's the way I look at it. I am just me and didn't realise how many people were interested in what I had to say or to come along and here me speak. All I ever wanted to do was pull on the blue (or red and black striped) jersey and just do my best. I can look back now and say that everything I wanted to achieve as a youngster came true.

There were a lot of stories fans related to me at the signing sessions and supporters club meetings that co-author David Clayton told me I should have included in the book but I've gone and bloody forgotten them all again since then. I blame him for not taking notes! I was chuffed with the people who came out in their hundreds and nobody came to take the mick or shout abuse at me. They were enjoyable evenings and I thank everyone who attended and hopefully they went away happy, knowing that I still hate Manchester United as much as I did in my playing days.

There was one incident that puzzled me about the media coverage, though. I was asked by the BBC to give my opinions about the Blues towards the end of the 2003/04 season when we were struggling. I chatted with Tony Gubba for Football Focus and gave my opinions and that was that. I never saw the edited version but I did get a lot of feedback from other people about it and from what I can muster, it didn't do me any favours. At the time, I did answer one question by saying that I felt the team at that time, would struggle in what is now The Championship. We were near the bottom of the table and that was my honest opinion, but I also said a lot of positive things about the club during the interview that seemingly never made it to the final broadcast.

Soon after, my book disappeared from the shelves in the City Store. My son Scott had gone in to have a look at how it was selling and couldn't find it anywhere. My publisher told me there'd been no re-order and that they should have had a few hundred copies left at the shop so I can only assume my comments caused offence and the book was removed. About 18 months ago, it re-appeared and happily is still there today. If I did offend anyone at the club, I'm surprised because I only ever want is the best for the Blues. I think somebody at the BBC did a number on me and I was probably set-up a bit, but I didn't lose any sleep over it. I couldn't do anything about it and the matter is closed now as far as I'm concerned but I'm glad the club were big enough to stock the book again and maybe realised my comments were taken the wrong way, thanks to clever editing.

Health-wise I'm doing OK. I even started playing golf again

a few months back, though I haven't been out since last summer and don't play regularly. My knee is no better but it could be some time before I have an operation so I just thought 'why not?' I played a few nine holes with Grant at Northenden but it did cause me some discomfort. All the injuries I sustained during my career simply caught up with me and in that respect, I paying my dues now. Grant is doing really well and now competing in tournaments and I think he'll make a good living from the game. He's a great coach, too, so I'm very proud of how things are going for him – he even gets on well with the former Manchester United players at Northenden – I might have to have a word with him about that!

Family life hasn't changed much but my mother passed away in the summer of 2005 and I'll miss her very much. Cherie and I are living together in a new house in Ashton and I seem to spend every waking hour stripping some wall or painting something or other. We've no new additions to the family, though Scott's little lad Thomas has definitely got something and just might make a footballer, one day. Sadly, the situation with my daughter Natalie has deteriorated further and I just cannot fathom her out at all.

Since the first edition came out, Brian Clough passed away. I had the utmost respect for Cloughie and having spoken to a few former Nottingham Forest and Derby County players, it just made me realise what a tremendous man he was. I spoke to him on several occasions and one of the biggest compliments he paid me was when he said he admired my attitude on the pitch. I was quite pleased with that and it would have been a privilege to play under him at some point – preferably as City manager! One of his best signings was former Blue, Ian Bowyer. Ian played a multitude of roles at City but Cloughie just played him on the left of midfield and he enjoyed a fantastic career with Forest. Many people thought of Clough as a bully but his players loved him and would have run through brick walls for him. His is a sad loss to football.

Back at City, there have been a few comings and goings worthy of note, starting with the departure of Kevin Keegan. I wasn't surprised when he left, just very disappointed because I've known him a long time and played alongside him for England. I chatted with him and chairman John Wardle at a Whitefield and Prestwich Blues meeting and it was great to catch up on old times. One thing I admired about Kevin as a player was his determination – he had talent, too, make no mistake, and when he went into management, he took that determination and desire along with him, though obviously fine-tuned for a totally different role. I think he was a success overall in management and I think had he utilised Stuart Pearce better as a coach on matchdays, things might have gone much better. I only ever saw Stuart on the sidelines barking instructions once during Kevin's reign and had he used Stuart's influence and passion to better effect on matchdays and perhaps the training pitch, it could only have benefited the team. I think Kevin might have left under different circumstances because I honestly feel it would have been better for him to have been sacked than resign. Resigning suggests you don't have the appetite any longer.

Stuart Pearce has been a breath of fresh air since taking over and you don't have to be a brain surgeon to see the effect he's already had on the players. You can see the players want to play for him and give their all and he wouldn't demand any less. Take Claudio Reyna – for me, he's improved the most under Pearce and I'd hold him as testament to Pearce's talent as a manager and now we're seeing the best of every player in the squad. I've always admired his attitude and rate him as one of the best players England have ever produced but it pisses me off that people still call him 'Psycho' – he's just focused, end of story and I can't stand it when people call him by that nickname. I'm hoping Stuart will help me out a little bit, too. The sooner I don't have to carry the mantle of being the last captain to win a major trophy, the better for all of us!

Nicolas Anelka moved on, too. I would have loved to have seen how he reacted to Pearce's style of management because his talent is frightening and in my book, he's as good as Thierry Henry. He seemed to plough a lonely furrow at times at City and, with the new improved team spirit and togetherness, I just wonder if we'd have seen an even better Nicolas Anelka than the one we witnessed. Many people have knocked his choice of club in Fenerbahce, but Turkish football is of a good standard.

Much as I miss Anelka, the departure that really gutted me was that of Shaun Wright-Phillips. In my opinion, Shaun was the best player in England for the past two years and it puzzles and saddens me to see him on the bench so often at Chelsea. When you pay £21million for a player, surely it's to play football as often as possible? I don't think it's a particularly good career move for Shaun and I know his roots are in London and I also know that when he does get the chance, he'll give his all as he always has done. But the momentum he had at City has stalled and I can't see him doing as well as he was doing with us at Chelsea. It's a sickener but I feel City have more than coped with his departure and the rest of the squad have responded extremely well. Look at Trevor Sinclair, Lee Croft and Stephen Ireland. They've all been doing well and maybe wouldn't have had their chance if Shaun had stayed.

Joey Barton is my favourite current player and I feel he should be in the England squad for Germany – let's face it, if Eriksson can pick Owen Hargreaves, Barton should make the squad with ease. He's had his off-field problems and I was glad that Pearce opted to help him rather than discard him. It would have been a loss to the club had he gone. Defensively I think Richard Dunne and Sylvain Distin have been magnificent and, for me, they are best central defensive pairing in the Premiership. Along with Barton, I feel these three players are the mainstay of the side.

Elsewhere, I see Colin Bell and Neil Young have released autobiographies recently. It still upsets me that Colin and Franny don't speak. After all we went through as a team, it still troubles me that things have ended they way they have, but I don't know the whole story. As for Youngy, it doesn't surprise me that he's had financial troubles because he never had two pennies to rub together when he was playing for City, either! He'd turn up in a new expensive suit each week and I think he was even a month in advance with his wages on occasions. I've not read either Colin's or Neil's books as yet, but I'll get around to them one day.

I see Rodney Marsh has put his foot in it again by making a joke about the Toon Army so soon after the Tsunami disaster on live television. I wasn't surprised Sky kicked him off Soccer Saturday for that remark and for someone to say something like that to an audience of millions I think you have to be absolutely brain-dead. Rodney isn't stupid and he should have known better.

I was also saddened to hear that Helen Turner had passed away. She was a wonderful character who everybody got on with and she'll be missed at the stadium. I have a couple of memories I'd like to share. I recall when Cherie was in the Manchester Royal Infirmary about to give birth to our first daughter, Natalie. I was playing the day she was born – we beat Chelsea 1-0 and, as I came out of the dressing room, Bernard Halford told me I was a dad and everything was fine. So Glyn Pardoe and me rushed to the hospital to see Cherie and the baby and obviously it was a very proud moment for me. As we left the hospital, Helen Turner was walking towards us and she looked concerned. "You're not injured are you?" she asked. I explained why I was there and she looked very happy about the baby and said it was "lovely". The next day when I came to visit, Cherie's hospital room looked like the inside of a florist. Helen had been in and put bunches of flowers everywhere and when I went out of the hospital, I made for her stall nearby. I asked how much I owed her and she said "Don't you dare think about giving me any money for those flowers!"

When we won the League Cup against Newcastle I spotted Helen in the crowd and jumped over the fence and took the trophy over to her and she lifted it aloft – still holding the bell! She came on the pitch with us and I know how that much meant to her but it was no more than she deserved for her loyalty over the years.

Well, that's it. I'm still at all the home matches, encouraging the lads and will continue to do so. I will literally be City till I die – and you can bank on that.

MIKE DOYLE – CAREER STATISTICS

Born Reddish Vale
25 November 1946

HONOURS

INTERNATIONAL
England 4(1), U23 8, Young Eng 1, FLge 2(1)

CLUB
ECWC (1970), Div1 (1968), Div2 (1966),
FAC (1969), FLC (1970,1976), ChSh (1968,1972)

MANCHESTER CITY
11 May 1962 (Apprentice)

	League		FA Cup		FL Cup		Europe		Other		Total	
1964-65	6		–		–						6	
1965-66	19 (1)	7	7	1	–						26 (1)	8
1966-67	14 (2)		5	1							19 (2)	1
1967-68	37 (1)	5	4		3						44 (1)	5
1968-69	40	5	7		3		2		1		53	5
1969-70	41	4	2		7	2	9	1	1		60	7
1970-71	37	5	3		1		7	1	2		50	6
1971-72	41	1	2		2				1	1	46	2
1972-73	38 (2)	1	5		1		2		1		47 (2)	1
1973-74	39	1	2		11				1		53	1
1974-75	42	1	1		2	1			3		48	2
1975-76	41	1	2		9	1			2		54	2
1976-77	33	1	4		1		2		2		42	1
1977-78	13 (1)		–		3		1				17 (1)	
TOTAL	441 (7)	32	44	2	43	4	23	2	14	1	565 (7)	41

STOKE CITY

5 June 1978 – fee: £50,000

	League	FA Cup	FL Cup	Europe	Other	Total
1978-79	41 *1*	1	4 *1*			46 2
1979-80	28	1	4			33
1980-81	38 *4*	2	–			40 *4*
1981-82	8	1	–			9
TOTAL	**115** *5*	**5**	**8** *1*			**128** *6*

BOLTON WANDERERS

28 January 1982 – fee: £10,000

	League	FA Cup	FL Cup	Europe	Other	Total
1981-82	10				10	
1982-83	30	2 –	2	2		32 *4*
TOTAL	**40**	**2** –	**2**	**2**		**42** *4*

ROCHDALE

August 1983 – Free

	League	FA Cup	FL Cup	Europe	Other	Total
1983-84	24	*1* 2	2		1	29 *1*

Retired 1984

TOTAL CAREER STATISTICS

League	FA Cup	FL Cup	Europe	Other	Total
620 (7) *40*	**51** *2*	**55** *7*	**23** *2*	**15** *1*	**764 (7)** *52*

* Substitute appearances in brackets.

* Goals scored in itallics.